Mometrix
TEST PREPARATION

I0866891

TerraNova®
NEXT
Grade 5 Mathematics Test Prep Guide

Written and edited by the Mometrix Test Preparation Team
Printed in the United States of America

TABLE OF CONTENTS

Introduction

Thank you for purchasing this resource! You have made the choice to prepare yourself for a test that could have a huge impact on your future, and this guide is designed to help you be fully ready for test day. Obviously, it's important to have a solid understanding of the test material, but you also need to be prepared for the unique environment and stressors of the test, so that you can perform to the best of your abilities.

For this purpose, the first section that appears in this guide is the **Success Strategies**. We've devoted countless hours to meticulously researching what works and what doesn't, and we've boiled down our findings to the most impactful steps you can take to improve your performance on the test. We start at the beginning with study planning and move through the preparation process, all the way to the testing strategies that will help you get the most out of what you know when you're finally sitting in front of the test.

We recommend that you start preparing for your test as far in advance as possible. However, if you've bought this guide as a last-minute study resource and only have a few days before your test, we recommend that you skip over the first two Success Strategies since they address a long-term study plan.

If you struggle with **test anxiety**, we strongly encourage you to check out our recommendations for how you can overcome it. Test anxiety is a formidable foe, but it can be beaten, and we want to make sure you have the tools you need to defeat it.

Strategy #1 - Plan Big, Study Small

There's a lot riding on your performance. If you want to ace this test, you're going to need to keep your skills sharp and the material fresh in your mind. You need a plan that lets you review everything you need to know while still fitting in your schedule. We'll break this strategy down into three categories.

Information Organization

Start with the information you already have: the official test outline. From this, you can make a complete list of all the concepts you need to cover before the test. Organize these concepts into groups that can be studied together, and create a list of any related vocabulary you need to learn so you can brush up on any difficult terms. You'll want to keep this vocabulary list handy once you actually start studying since you may need to add to it along the way.

Time Management

Once you have your set of study concepts, decide how to spread them out over the time you have left before the test. Break your study plan into small, clear goals so you have a manageable task for each day and know exactly what you're doing. Then just focus on one small step at a time. When you manage your time this way, you don't need to spend hours at a time studying. Studying a small block of content for a short period each day helps you retain information better and avoid stressing over how much you have left to do. You can relax knowing that you have a plan to cover everything in time. In order for this strategy to be effective though, you have to start studying early and stick to your schedule. Avoid the exhaustion and futility that comes from last-minute cramming!

Study Environment

The environment you study in has a big impact on your learning. Studying in a coffee shop, while probably more enjoyable, is not likely to be as fruitful as studying in a quiet room. It's important to keep distractions to a minimum. You're only planning to study for a short block of time, so make the most of it. Don't pause to check your phone or get up to find a snack. It's also important to **avoid multitasking**. Research has consistently shown that multitasking will make your studying dramatically less effective. Your study area should also be comfortable and well-lit so you don't have the distraction of straining your eyes or sitting on an uncomfortable chair.

The time of day you study is also important. You want to be rested and alert. Don't wait until just before bedtime. Study when you'll be most likely to comprehend and remember. Even better, if you know what time of day your test will be, set that time aside for study. That way your brain will be used to working on that subject at that specific time and you'll have a better chance of recalling information.

Finally, it can be helpful to team up with others who are studying for the same test. Your actual studying should be done in as isolated an environment as possible, but the work of organizing the information and setting up the study plan can be divided up. In between study sessions, you can discuss with your teammates the concepts that you're all studying and quiz each other on the details. Just be sure that your teammates are as serious about the test as you are. If you find that your study time is being replaced with social time, you might need to find a new team.

Strategy #2 – Make Your Studying Count

You're devoting a lot of time and effort to preparing for this test, so you want to be absolutely certain it will pay off. This means doing more than just reading the content and hoping you can remember it on test day. It's important to make every minute of study count. There are two main areas you can focus on to make your studying count.

Retention

It doesn't matter how much time you study if you can't remember the material. You need to make sure you are retaining the concepts. To check your retention of the information you're learning, try recalling it at later times with minimal prompting. Try carrying around flashcards and glance at one or two from time to time or ask a friend who's also studying for the test to quiz you.

To enhance your retention, look for ways to put the information into practice so that you can apply it rather than simply recalling it. If you're using the information in practical ways, it will be much easier to remember. Similarly, it helps to solidify a concept in your mind if you're not only reading it to yourself but also explaining it to someone else. Ask a friend to let you teach them about a concept you're a little shaky on (or speak aloud to an imaginary audience if necessary). As you try to summarize, define, give examples, and answer your friend's questions, you'll understand the concepts better and they will stay with you longer. Finally, step back for a big picture view and ask yourself how each piece of information fits with the whole subject. When you link the different concepts together and see them working together as a whole, it's easier to remember the individual components.

Finally, practice showing your work on any multi-step problems, even if you're just studying. Writing out each step you take to solve a problem will help solidify the process in your mind, and you'll be more likely to remember it during the test.

Modality

Modality simply refers to the means or method by which you study. Choosing a study modality that fits your own individual learning style is crucial. No two people learn best in exactly the same way, so it's important to know your strengths and use them to your advantage.

For example, if you learn best by visualization, focus on visualizing a concept in your mind and draw an image or a diagram. Try color-coding your notes, illustrating them, or creating symbols that will trigger your mind to recall a learned concept. If you learn best by hearing or discussing information, find a study partner who learns the same way or read aloud to yourself. Think about how to put the information in your own words. Imagine that you are giving a lecture on the topic and record yourself so you can listen to it later.

For any learning style, flashcards can be helpful. Organize the information so you can take advantage of spare moments to review. Underline key words or phrases. Use different colors for different categories. Mnemonic devices (such as creating a short list in which every item starts with the same letter) can also help with retention. Find what works best for you and use it to store the information in your mind most effectively and easily.

Strategy #3 – Practice the Right Way

Your success on test day depends not only on how many hours you put into preparing, but also on whether you prepared the right way. It's good to check along the way to see if your studying is paying off. One of the most effective ways to do this is by taking practice tests to evaluate your progress. Practice tests are useful because they show exactly where you need to improve. Every time you take a practice test, pay special attention to these three groups of questions:

- The questions you got wrong
- The questions you had to guess on, even if you guessed right
- The questions you found difficult or slow to work through

This will show you exactly what your weak areas are, and where you need to devote more study time. Ask yourself why each of these questions gave you trouble. Was it because you didn't understand the material? Was it because you didn't remember the vocabulary? Do you need more repetitions on this type of question to build speed and confidence? Dig into those questions and figure out how you can strengthen your weak areas as you go back to review the material.

Additionally, many practice tests have a section explaining the answer choices. It can be tempting to read the explanation and think that you now have a good understanding of the concept. However, an explanation likely only covers part of the question's broader context. Even if the explanation makes perfect sense, **go back and investigate** every concept related to the question until you're positive you have a thorough understanding.

As you go along, keep in mind that the practice test is just that: practice. Memorizing these questions and answers will not be very helpful on the actual test because it is unlikely to have any of the same exact questions. If you only know the right answers to the sample questions, you won't be prepared for the real thing. **Study the concepts** until you understand them fully, and then you'll be able to answer any question that shows up on the test.

It's important to wait on the practice tests until you're ready. If you take a test on your first day of study, you may be overwhelmed by the amount of material covered and how much you need to learn. Work up to it gradually.

On test day, you'll need to be prepared for answering questions, managing your time, and using the test-taking strategies you've learned. It's a lot to balance, like a mental marathon that will have a big impact on your future. Like training for a marathon, you'll need to start slowly and work your way up. When test day arrives, you'll be ready.

Start with the strategies you've read in the first two Success Strategies—plan your course and study in the way that works best for you. If you have time, consider using multiple study resources to get different approaches to the same concepts. It can be helpful to see difficult concepts from more than one angle. Then find a good source for practice tests. Many times, the test website will suggest potential study resources or provide sample tests.

Practice Test Strategy

If you're able to find at least three practice tests, we recommend this strategy:

Untimed and Open-Book Practice

Take the first test with no time constraints and with your notes and study guide handy. Take your time and focus on applying the strategies you've learned.

Timed and Open-Book Practice

Take the second practice test open-book as well, but set a timer and practice pacing yourself to finish in time.

Timed and Closed-Book Practice

Take any other practice tests as if it were test day. Set a timer and put away your study materials. Sit at a table or desk in a quiet room, imagine yourself at the testing center, and answer questions as quickly and accurately as possible.

Keep repeating timed and closed-book tests on a regular basis until you run out of practice tests or it's time for the actual test. Your mind will be ready for the schedule and stress of test day, and you'll be able to focus on recalling the material you've learned.

Strategy #4 – Pace Yourself

Once you're fully prepared for the material on the test, your biggest challenge on test day will be managing your time. Just knowing that the clock is ticking can make you panic even if you have plenty of time left. Work on pacing yourself so you can build confidence against the time constraints of the exam. Pacing is a difficult skill to master, especially in a high-pressure environment, so **practice is vital**.

Set time expectations for your pace based on how much time is available. For example, if a section has 60 questions and the time limit is 30 minutes, you know you have to average 30 seconds or less per question in order to answer them all. Although 30 seconds is the hard limit, set 25 seconds per question as your goal, so you reserve extra time to spend on harder questions. When you budget extra time for the harder questions, you no longer have any reason to stress when those questions take longer to answer.

Don't let this time expectation distract you from working through the test at a calm, steady pace, but keep it in mind so you don't spend too much time on any one question. Recognize that taking extra time on one question you don't understand may keep you from answering two that you do understand later in the test. If your time limit for a question is up and you're still not sure of the answer, mark it and move on, and come back to it later if the time and the test format allow. If the testing format doesn't allow you to return to earlier questions, just make an educated guess; then put it out of your mind and move on.

On the easier questions, be careful not to rush. It may seem wise to hurry through them so you have more time for the challenging ones, but it's not worth missing one if you know the concept and just didn't take the time to read the question fully. Work efficiently but make sure you understand the question and have looked at all of the answer choices, since more than one may seem right at first.

Even if you're paying attention to the time, you may find yourself a little behind at some point. You should speed up to get back on track, but do so wisely. Don't panic; just take a few seconds less on each question until you're caught up. Don't guess without thinking, but do look through the answer choices and eliminate any you know are wrong. If you can get down to two choices, it is often worthwhile to guess from those. Once you've chosen an answer, move on and don't dwell on any that you skipped or had to hurry through. If a question was taking too long, chances are it was one of the harder ones, so you weren't as likely to get it right anyway.

On the other hand, if you find yourself getting ahead of schedule, it may be beneficial to slow down a little. The more quickly you work, the more likely you are to make a careless mistake that will affect your score. You've budgeted time for each question, so don't be afraid to spend that time. Practice an efficient but careful pace to get the most out of the time you have.

Test-Taking Strategies

This section contains a list of test-taking strategies that you may find helpful as you work through the test. By taking what you know and applying logical thought, you can maximize your chances of answering any question correctly!

It is very important to realize that every question is different and every person is different: no single strategy will work on every question, and no single strategy will work for every person. That's why we've included all of them here, so you can try them out and determine which ones work best for different types of questions and which ones work best for you.

Question Strategies

✓ Read Carefully

Read the question and the answer choices carefully. Don't miss the question because you misread the terms. You have plenty of time to read each question thoroughly and make sure you understand what is being asked. Yet a happy medium must be attained, so don't waste too much time. You must read carefully and efficiently.

✓ Contextual Clues

Look for contextual clues. If the question includes a word you are not familiar with, look at the immediate context for some indication of what the word might mean. Contextual clues can often give you all the information you need to decipher the meaning of an unfamiliar word. Even if you can't determine the meaning, you may be able to narrow down the possibilities enough to make a solid guess at the answer to the question.

✓ Prefixes

If you're having trouble with a word in the question or answer choices, try dissecting it. Take advantage of every clue that the word might include. Prefixes can be a huge help. Usually, they allow you to determine a basic meaning. *Pre-* means before, *post-* means after, *pro-* is positive, *de-* is negative. From prefixes, you can get an idea of the general meaning of the word and try to put it into context.

✓ Hedge Words

Watch out for critical hedge words, such as *likely, may, can, often, almost, mostly, usually, generally, rarely,* and *sometimes.* Question writers insert these hedge phrases to cover every possibility. Often an answer choice will be wrong simply because it leaves no room for exception. Be on guard for answer choices that have definitive words such as *exactly* and *always.*

✓ Switchback Words

Stay alert for *switchbacks.* These are the words and phrases frequently used to alert you to shifts in thought. The most common switchback words are *but, although,* and *however.* Others include *nevertheless, on the other hand, even though, while, in spite of, despite,* and *regardless of.* Switchback words are important to catch because they can change the direction of the question or an answer choice.

☑ Face Value

When in doubt, use common sense. Accept the situation in the problem at face value. Don't read too much into it. These problems will not require you to make wild assumptions. If you have to go beyond creativity and warp time or space in order to have an answer choice fit the question, then you should move on and consider the other answer choices. These are normal problems rooted in reality. The applicable relationship or explanation may not be readily apparent, but it is there for you to figure out. Use your common sense to interpret anything that isn't clear.

Answer Choice Strategies

☑ Answer Selection

The most thorough way to pick an answer choice is to identify and eliminate wrong answers until only one is left, then confirm it is the correct answer. Sometimes an answer choice may immediately seem right, but be careful. The test writers will usually put more than one reasonable answer choice on each question, so take a second to read all of them and make sure that the other choices are not equally obvious. As long as you have time left, it is better to read every answer choice than to pick the first one that looks right without checking the others.

☑ Answer Choice Families

An answer choice family consists of two (in rare cases, three) answer choices that are very similar in construction and cannot all be true at the same time. If you see two answer choices that are direct opposites or parallels, one of them is usually the correct answer. For instance, if one answer choice says that quantity *x* increases and another either says that quantity *x* decreases (opposite) or says that quantity *y* increases (parallel), then those answer choices would fall into the same family. An answer choice that doesn't match the construction of the answer choice family is more likely to be incorrect. Most questions will not have answer choice families, but when they do appear, you should be prepared to recognize them.

☑ Eliminate Answers

Eliminate answer choices as soon as you realize they are wrong, but make sure you consider all possibilities. If you are eliminating answer choices and realize that the last one you are left with is also wrong, don't panic. Start over and consider each choice again. There may be something you missed the first time that you will realize on the second pass.

☑ Avoid Fact Traps

Don't be distracted by an answer choice that is factually true but doesn't answer the question. You are looking for the choice that answers the question. Stay focused on what the question is asking for so you don't accidentally pick an answer that is true but incorrect. Always go back to the question and make sure the answer choice you've selected actually answers the question and is not merely a true statement.

☑ Extreme Statements

In general, you should avoid answers that put forth extreme actions as standard practice or proclaim controversial ideas as established fact. An answer choice that states the "process should be used in certain situations, if..." is much more likely to be correct than one that states the "process should be discontinued completely." The first is a calm rational statement and doesn't even make a definitive, uncompromising stance, using a hedge word *if* to provide wiggle room, whereas the second choice is far more extreme.

⊘ BENCHMARK

As you read through the answer choices and you come across one that seems to answer the question well, mentally select that answer choice. This is not your final answer, but it's the one that will help you evaluate the other answer choices. The one that you selected is your benchmark or standard for judging each of the other answer choices. Every other answer choice must be compared to your benchmark. That choice is correct until proven otherwise by another answer choice beating it. If you find a better answer, then that one becomes your new benchmark. Once you've decided that no other choice answers the question as well as your benchmark, you have your final answer.

⊘ PREDICT THE ANSWER

Before you even start looking at the answer choices, it is often best to try to predict the answer. When you come up with the answer on your own, it is easier to avoid distractions and traps because you will know exactly what to look for. The right answer choice is unlikely to be word-for-word what you came up with, but it should be a close match. Even if you are confident that you have the right answer, you should still take the time to read each option before moving on.

General Strategies

⊘ TOUGH QUESTIONS

If you are stumped on a problem or it appears too hard or too difficult, don't waste time. Move on! Remember though, if you can quickly check for obviously incorrect answer choices, your chances of guessing correctly are greatly improved. Before you completely give up, at least try to knock out a couple of possible answers. Eliminate what you can and then guess at the remaining answer choices before moving on.

⊘ CHECK YOUR WORK

Since you will probably not know every term listed and the answer to every question, it is important that you get credit for the ones that you do know. Don't miss any questions through careless mistakes. If at all possible, try to take a second to look back over your answer selection and make sure you've selected the correct answer choice and haven't made a costly careless mistake (such as marking an answer choice that you didn't mean to mark). This quick double check should more than pay for itself in caught mistakes for the time it costs.

⊘ PACE YOURSELF

It's easy to be overwhelmed when you're looking at a page full of questions; your mind is confused and full of random thoughts, and the clock is ticking down faster than you would like. Calm down and maintain the pace that you have set for yourself. Especially as you get down to the last few minutes of the test, don't let the small numbers on the clock make you panic. As long as you are on track by monitoring your pace, you are guaranteed to have time for each question.

⊘ DON'T RUSH

It is very easy to make errors when you are in a hurry. Maintaining a fast pace in answering questions is pointless if it makes you miss questions that you would have gotten right otherwise. Test writers like to include distracting information and wrong answers that seem right. Taking a little extra time to avoid careless mistakes can make all the difference in your test score. Find a pace that allows you to be confident in the answers that you select.

✓ Keep Moving

Panicking will not help you pass the test, so do your best to stay calm and keep moving. Taking deep breaths and going through the answer elimination steps you practiced can help to break through a stress barrier and keep your pace.

Final Notes

The combination of a solid foundation of content knowledge and the confidence that comes from practicing your plan for applying that knowledge is the key to maximizing your performance on test day. As your foundation of content knowledge is built up and strengthened, you'll find that the strategies included in this chapter become more and more effective in helping you quickly sift through the distractions and traps of the test to isolate the correct answer.

Now that you're preparing to move forward into the test content chapters of this book, be sure to keep your goal in mind. As you read, think about how you will be able to apply this information on the test. If you've already seen sample questions for the test and you have an idea of the question format and style, try to come up with questions of your own that you can answer based on what you're reading. This will give you valuable practice applying your knowledge in the same ways you can expect to on test day.

Good luck and good studying!

Operations & Algebraic Thinking

Expressions and Equations

Numerical expressions are mathematical phrases with numbers, operations, and/or variables. Expressions do not have an equal sign. Equations, on the other hand, show two mathematical expressions are equivalent or equal using an equal sign.

Expressions and equations can be expressed through mathematical descriptions. These can then be written into numerical forms. For example, two less than forty-three can be written as $43 - 2$. This is an expression. Furthermore, the description that the quotient of fifty-six and eight is seven can also be written as $56 \div 8 = 7$. This is an equation.

To determine whether an equation is true or false, simplify both sides of the equation. If both expressions are not equivalent, then the equation is false. For example, $5 + 3 \times 4 = 17$ is true, but $6 + 9 \div 3 = 5$ is false. This is shown below.

$$\begin{aligned} 5 + 3 \times 4 &= 17 \\ 5 + 12 &= 17 \\ 17 &= 17 \end{aligned}$$

$$\begin{aligned} 6 + 9 \div 3 &= 5 \\ 6 + 3 &= 5 \\ 9 &\neq 5 \end{aligned}$$

Word Problems and the Four Operations

Solving problems using all operations might include answering word problems that involve more than one step or operation. When you encounter a problem that describes a situation, the best way to approach these problems is to identify the information that is known, identify the information that is unknown, and draw a picture.

Example

Marlo is planning a trip to an amusement park. She only has $100 to spend. Marlo is planning to bring 3 other people, and each ticket costs $18. Marlo wants to use the remaining money to buy pictures taken on some of the rides. If each picture costs $6, how many pictures can Marlo buy?

The first step to solve this problem is by identifying the known and the unknowns. Let's start with what is known. It is known that a total of 4 tickets will be purchased if you include Marlo's ticket. It is also known that Marlo only has $100 to spend in total. The final known is that each picture costs $8.

Now, what is the unknown? In this problem, the unknown is how many pictures Marlo can buy. This is what needs to be found.

The expression $100 - 4 \times 18$ will determine how much money Marlo has remaining after buying all the tickets. Since 4 times 18 is equal to 72, subtract 72 from 100. The remaining amount that Marlo has is \$28.

Since each picture costs \$6, the expression $28 \div 6$ will determine how many pictures Marlo can purchase. Since 6 does not fit evenly into 28, and she cannot buy a partial picture, Marlo will not use her money entirely. $28 \div 6 = 4\frac{2}{3}$, so Marlo can only buy 4 pictures. She will have \$4 remaining after buying all four amusement park tickets and 4 pictures since 6 times 4 is 24 and 28 minus 24 is equal to 4.

Multi-Step Problems with Variables

Multi-step word problems can be solved algebraically. In general, equations will consist of variables, coefficients, and constants. **Variables** are letters that represent unknown values. **Coefficients** are located in front of variables and signal multiplication. For example, $2x$ means 2 multiplied by the variable x. **Constants** are numbers that are not attached to variables. This means that constants are fixed values that do not change, regardless of the value of the variable.

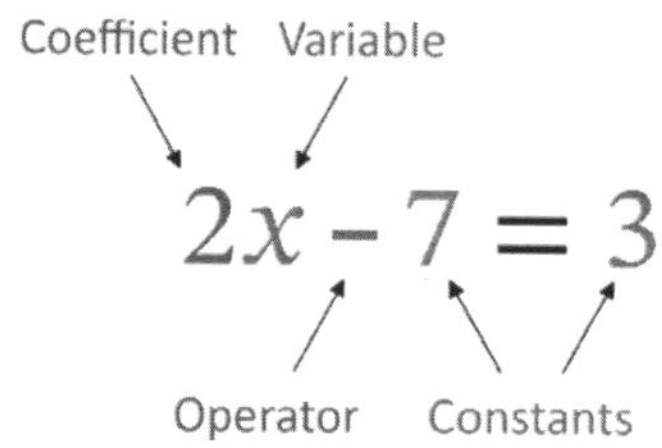

An equation is solved when the value of the variable is calculated. For example, if the equation states that $45 = 9 \times T$, the value of T is 5. This is considered a **one-step equation** because it is solved by dividing both sides of the equation by 9, which requires only one step. However, many equations require more than one step to solve. Consider the following scenario.

The temperature of water in a pool starts at 82°. The temperature rises 0.6 degrees every hour. Right now, the water temperature is 85°. How many hours have passed?

The word problem can be solved using an algebraic equation. Start by stating what is known.

- The water temperature is initially 82°.
- The temperature rises 0.6° each hour.
- Now the water temperature is 85°.

Then identify the unknown. Here, the unknown is the number of hours that have passed. Since the number of hours is unknown, use h as the unknown variable. The goal is to set up a multi-step equation that can be solved for h.

The problem states that the water temperature will eventually be 85°, so start the equation with $85 =$.

$$85 =$$

The problem also states that the temperature will rise 0.6 degrees each hour. This can be represented as $(0.6) \times (h)$.

$$85 = (0.6) \times (h)$$

Since the water temperature starts at 82°, $(0.6) \times (h)$ should be added to 82°.

The result is the following equation.

$$85 = (0.6) \times (h) + 82$$

Solve for the variable h by subtracting 82 from both sides, and then use long division to divide by 0.6.

$$82 + (0.6) \times (h) = 85$$

$$(0.6) \times (h) = 3$$

$$h = 5$$

This means that 5 hours have passed.

EXAMPLE

Write and solve an equation to solve the following problem.

A school is taking a field trip. There are 331 students attending the field trip. 6 school busses are filled with an equal number of students, and 7 students will ride their bike to the field trip. How many students will be in each school bus?

54 students. $331 = 6b + 7$

Start by listing all the relevant facts.

- The total number of students is 331.
- 6 busses will be full, with an equal number of students on each bus.
- 7 students will ride their bikes

The equation will follow the format of Total Students = Bus Riders + Bikers. Fill in what is provided.

The total number of students is 331, so start the equation with $331 =$.

$$331 =$$

An equal number of bus riders will be placed on 6 buses. It is unknown how many riders will be on each bus. A variable can be substituted in for this unknown value. Use the variable b to represent the unknown number of riders on each bus. There are 6 buses, and b number of students on each bus. The expression $6 \times b$ or $6b$ can be used to describe "six buses with an equal number of students."

$$331 = 6(b)$$

The number of bikers is 7, so add a +7 to the end of the equation.

$$331 = 6(b) + 7$$

Now use the equation to solve for the unknown variable, b. The equation is solved in two steps. Subtract 7 from both sides, and then divide both sides by 6. These two steps are considered "inverse operations." Subtracting 7 is the inverse of adding 7, and dividing by 6 is the inverse of multiplying by 6.

$$331 = 6b + 7$$

$$324 = 6b$$

$$54 = b$$

This means that there will be 54 students on each bus.

EXAMPLE

Write and solve an equation to solve the following problem.

You purchased 4 cups of coffee and left a $5 bill as a tip. You spent $25 altogether. How much did each cup of coffee cost?

$5 per cup of coffee. $25 = 4c + 5$

Generate a list of all relevant information within the problem.

- You spent $25 altogether.
- You purchased 4 cups of coffee.
- You left a tip of $5.

Set up an equation that represents the scenario. The equation will follow the format of

$25 = Cost of Coffee + $5 tip. Now, substitute the values that are provided. The total cost is $25, so start the equation with $25 =$.

$$25 =$$

4 cups of coffee were purchased, but the cost of each cup is unknown. Substitute a variable in for the unknown cost. Consider the variable c to represent cost. 4 cups of coffee were purchased, at a cost of c, so the expression $4 \times c$, or $4c$ can be used in the equation.

$$25 = 4(c)$$

The tip was $5, so add a $+5$ to the end of the equation.

$$25 = 4c + 5$$

Now use "inverse operations" to isolate the variable, c. The inverse of adding 5 is subtracting 5, so subtract 5 from both sides. The inverse of multiplying by 4 is dividing by 4.

$$25 = 4c + 5$$

$$20 = 4c$$

$$5 = c$$

This means that each cup of coffee cost $5.

Numerical Patterns Based on Equations

Equations in the form $y = ax$ or $y = x + a$ can be useful when looking for **patterns** or solving for **unknown values**. For example, consider the following scenario.

A cherry tree grows 7 inches each year. If the tree was planted as a seed, how tall will the tree be after 5 years?

This represents a $y = ax$ scenario because the height of the tree is calculated by multiplying the number of years by 7. In this case, $y = ax$ is represented as

height $= 7 \times$ years. The equation $y = 7 \times 5$ can be solved to calculate the height after 5 years. $y = 7 \times 5 = 35$, so the tree will be 35 inches after 5 years.

This equation, or rule, can be used to create a pattern. For example, plot the tree's height each year in a table. Notice how the height increases by 7 inches each year. The yearly height pattern can be described as 0, 7, 14, 21, 28, 35 and so on.

Year	0	1	2	3	4	5
Height (in.)	0	7	14	21	28	35

These data points can also be displayed in a graph. For example, plot the years on the x-axis, and the heights on the y-axis. Each data point will form an ordered pair. Notice how the pattern forms a line that increases at a steady rate. This is known as a linear graph.

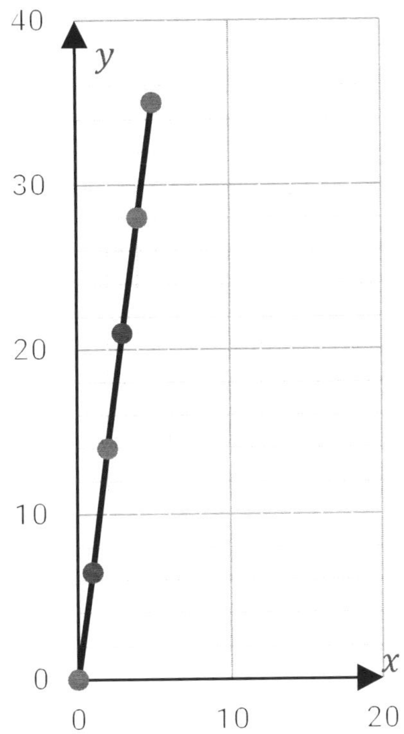

Similarly, $y = x + a$ equations can be used to generate numerical patterns. Consider the following scenario.

Craig is 2 years older than his younger brother Sam. How old will Sam be when Craig is 20?

This represents a $y = x + a$ scenario because Craig's age can be calculated by adding 2 to Sam's age. In other words, $C = 2 + S$. When Sam is 18, Craig will be 2 more than 18, or 20. This equation, or rule, can be represented graphically. Each pair of data points will form an ordered pair on the graph. For example, when Sam is 16, Craig is 18. When Sam is 17, Craig is 19. When Sam is 18, Craig is 20. The pattern forms a line that rises at a steady rate. This is known as a linear equation.

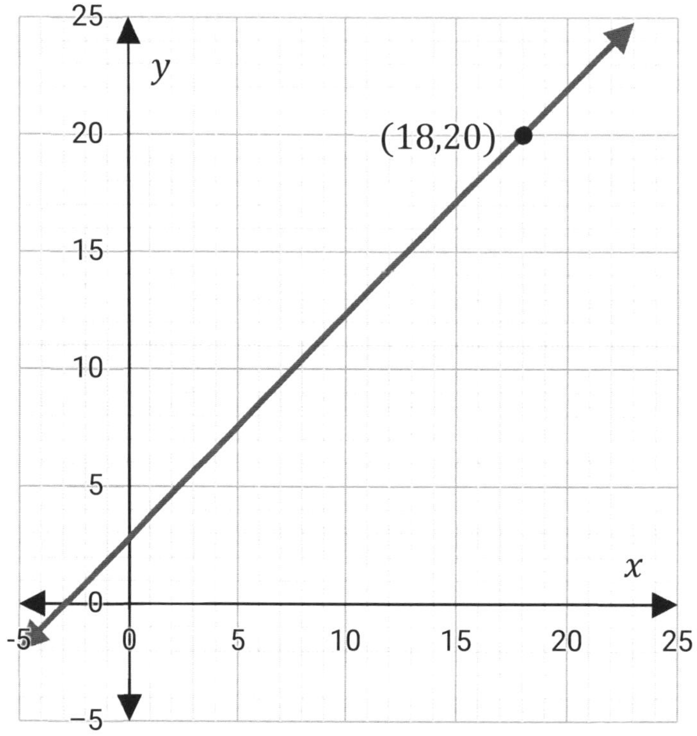

Additive and Multiplicative Relationships

Pattens can be additive or multiplicative. **Additive relationships** add the same number to the x-value to calculate the corresponding y-value. These equations take the form $y = x + a$. For example, $y = x + 8$ is additive. **Multiplicative relationships** multiply the x-value by the same number to calculate the corresponding y-value. For example, $y = 4x$ is multiplicative. It is important to be able to determine if a relationship is additive or multiplicative based on a table or a graph.

For example, the table below shows x- and y-values. Notice how each y-value is 1 more than its corresponding x-value. In other words, $y = x + 1$. This table represents an additive relationship.

x	y
4	5
6	7
8	9
12	13

The table below shows x- and y-values where each y-value is twice the value of x. This can be expressed as $y = 2x$. This represents a multiplicative relationship.

x	6	7	8	9
y	12	14	16	18

When determining if a graph is additive or multiplicative, look at the relationship between the x- and y-variables. For example, in the graph below, there are two ordered pairs plotted: (1,3) and (4,12). Notice how each y-value is 3 times as large as its corresponding x-value.

- (1,3): 3 is 3 times larger than 1.
- (4,12): 12 is 3 times larger than 4.

This means the graph is multiplicative.

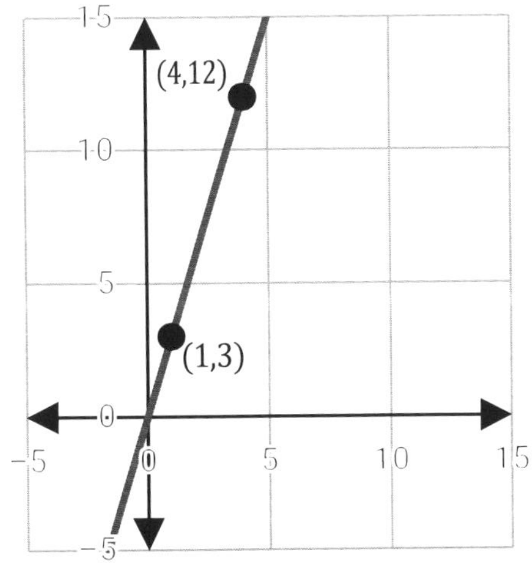

Input-Output Tables

Expressions, such as $5m$, can be displayed in an **input-output table**. For example, in the expression $5m$, when $m = 1$, the expression becomes $5(1)$ which simplifies to 5. When $m = 2$, the expression becomes $5(2)$ which simplifies to 10. The pattern continues.

This can be shown with an input-output table. The **input value** is m, and the **output value** is determined when the expression is evaluated.

Input (m)	1	2	3	4	5
Output ($5m$)	5	10	15	20	25

Notice how each input value increases by 1, and each output value increases by 5.

When an input-output table represents a consistent pattern, the pattern is referred to as a **rule**. The rule in this example is, "multiply by five." A rule makes it possible to determine unknown values in an input-output table. For example, if $m = 15$, the output is determined by multiplying 15 and 5: $15 \times 5 = 75$. When $m = 5$, the output is 75.

Example

Complete the input-output table relating the number of bikes and the total number of wheels. Write a rule to describe the relationship.

Number of Bikes	Number of Wheels
1	2
2	
4	
6	
10	

The relationship between the number of bikes and the number of wheels can be described with the following "rule": $w = 2b$, where w represents the total number of wheels, and b represents the number of bikes. The total number of wheels is calculated by multiplying the number of bikes by 2.

Number of Bikes	Number of Wheels
1	2
2	4
4	8
6	12
10	20

Example

Complete the input-output table based on the following rule. RULE: Add 19 to the input.

Input	Output
4	
9	
16	
19	
25	

The rule states "add 19 to the input". This means that 19 will be added to every input value to calculate the corresponding output value.

Input	Output
4	23
9	28
16	35
19	38
25	44

Parentheses and Brackets in Numerical Expressions

Parentheses and brackets are considered **grouping symbols**. These symbols indicate which sections of a numerical expression should be simplified first. Think of parentheses and brackets as layers of an onion. Parentheses are inner layers and brackets are outer layers. When solving expressions, find the middle of the onion and simplify that first. Then gradually work your way to the outermost layer using the order of operations.

Parentheses: ( )

Brackets: [ ]

Parentheses and brackets are used to separate expressions from other terms. For example, consider the expression $[3(2 \times 2 + 8 \times 2)] \div [5 \times 2 + 10]$. Look for the "center of the onion." Look for the math inside the parentheses and simplify this first. $(2 \times 2 + 8 \times 2)$ becomes $4 + 16$ and then 20. The expression is now $[3(20)] \div [5 \times 2 + 10]$. Now move to the math inside of the brackets. Look at the bracket on the left. $[3(20)]$ indicates 3×20, which simplifies to 60. The expression is now $60 \div [5 \times 2 + 10]$. Move to the brackets on the right. $[5 \times 2 + 10]$ becomes $[10 + 10]$ and then 20. Now the expression is $60 \div 30$, which simplifies to 2. By solving the parentheses and brackets first, and following the order of operations, the numerical expression $[3(2 \times 2 + 8 \times 2)] \div [5 \times 2 + 10]$ simplifies to 2.

> **Review Video: Mathematical Parentheses**
> Visit mometrix.com/academy and enter code: 978600

Order of Operations

Follow the order of operations (PEMDAS) when simplifying numerical expressions.

P- parentheses and grouping symbols
E- exponents
M/D- multiplication/division (left to right)
A/S- addition/subtraction (left to right)

For example, consider the numerical expression $2[(9 + 21) \div 6]$. Start by simplifying the math inside the parentheses. $(9 + 21)$ simplifies to 30.

$$2[30 \div 6]$$

Now simplify the math inside the brackets. $[30 \div 6]$ simplifies to 5.

$$2[5]$$

Multiply 2 by 5. The result is 10, so $2[(9 + 21) \div 6]$ simplifies to 10.

> **Review Video: Order of Operations**
> Visit mometrix.com/academy and enter code: 259675

Example

Simplify the expression: $(4 \times 5 + 100 \div 4) - 15$

30

Use the order of operations when simplifying numerical expressions. This is often referred to as PEMDAS. In the expression $(4 \times 5 + 100 \div 4) - 15$, start by simplifying the math within the parentheses. Remember to follow the order of operations inside parentheses, so complete multiplication and division in order from left to right before adding. $4 \times 5 = 20$ and $100 \div 4 = 25$.

$$(20 + 25) - 15$$

Now, add.

$$45 - 15$$

Finally, subtract.

$$45 - 15 = 30$$

EXAMPLE

$$\frac{[(0.75 + 10) - 2 \times 5] + 8.25}{9}$$

When simplifying expressions, solve the math within grouping elements first. Remember to follow the order of operations within grouping elements, so first simplify the parentheses inside the brackets.

$$[10.75 - 2 \times 5] + 8.25$$

Then, simplify the multiplication inside the brackets.

$$[10.75 - 10] + 8.25$$

Now simplify the subtraction within the brackets.

$$0.75 + 8.25$$

Finally, add.

$$0.75 + 8.25 = 9$$

Numbers and Operations in Base Ten

Decimal Values and Notation

Decimal values can be split apart based on their place value in **expanded notation**. For example, the value 593.217 can be expanded by writing the value as the sum of its place values.

Consider the number 593.217:

5 represents 5 groups of 100.
9 represents 9 groups of 10
3 represents 3 groups of 1.
2 represents 2 groups of $\frac{1}{10}$.
1 represents 1 group of $\frac{1}{100}$.
7 represents 7 groups of $\frac{1}{1,000}$.

$$593.217 = 500 + 90 + 3 + 0.2 + 0.01 + 0.007$$

$500 + 90 + 3 + 0.2 + 0.01 + 0.007$ is considered expanded form.

Decimal values can also be displayed using **word notation**. The word form of this decimal value is five hundred ninety-three and two hundred seventeen thousandths.

Multiplying by 10 and 100

When multiplying by 10, the decimal point moves **one place** to the **right**. When multiplying by 100, the decimal point moves **two places** to the **right**. The pattern continues for each multiple of 10. This is a convenient way to multiply numbers by powers of 10. For example, notice the decimal movement in the following examples:

$$45.62 \times 10 = 456.2$$

$$45.62 \times 100 = 4,562.0$$

The same pattern can be seen when multiplying whole numbers. Any whole number can be expressed as a decimal. Think about where the decimal point is in the number 50. Sometimes the decimal point is not written for whole numbers, but it's technically there. 50 has a "decimal" to the right of the ones place. Remember, a decimal separates the ones place from the tenths place. 50 is equal to 50.0.

$$50.0 \times 10 = 500.0$$

Notice how the decimal moves one place to the right.

$$50.0 \times 100 = 5,000.0$$

Notice how the decimal moves two places to the right.

Multiplying and Dividing by One-Tenth and One-Hundredth

When multiplying by $\frac{1}{10}$, the decimal point moves **one place** to the **left**. When multiplying by $\frac{1}{100}$, the decimal point moves **two places** to the **left**. The pattern continues for every denominator that is a multiple of 10. This is the opposite of multiplying by powers of 10. When multiplying by a fraction of a whole, the product should have a lesser value. For example, notice the decimal movement in the following examples:

$$45.6 \times \frac{1}{10} = 4.56$$

$$45.6 \times \frac{1}{100} = 0.456$$

On the other hand, when dividing a number by $\frac{1}{10}$, the decimal point moves **one place** to the **right**. When dividing by $\frac{1}{100}$, the decimal point moves **two places** to the **right**. The pattern continues for every denominator that is a multiple of 10. This is the opposite of dividing by powers of 10. When dividing by a fraction of a whole, the product should have a greater value. For example, notice the decimal movement in the following examples:

$$45.6 \div \frac{1}{10} = 456.0$$

$$45.6 \div \frac{1}{100} = 4560.0$$

The same pattern can be seen when multiplying and dividing whole numbers. Any whole number can be expressed as a decimal. Think about where the decimal point is in the number 50. Sometimes the decimal point is not written for whole numbers, but it's technically there. 50 has a "decimal" to the right of the ones place. Remember, a decimal separates the ones place from the tenths place. 50 is equal to 50.0.

$$50.0 \times \frac{1}{10} = 5.0$$

Notice how the decimal moves one place to the left.

$$50.0 \div \frac{1}{100} = 5000.0$$

Notice how the decimal moves two places to the right.

Comparing Decimal Values

When comparing decimal values, it is important to remember that digits are compared from left to right according to **place value**. For example, when comparing the values 146.079 and 146.792, start at the left and move to the right one digit at a time, until the digits differ.

146.079 and 146.792 both have 1 in the hundreds place.

146.079 and 146.792 both have 4 in the tens place.

146.079 and 146.792 both have 6 in the ones place.

146.079 and 146.792 do not have the same value in the tenths place. The first number has 0 tenths, and the second number has 7 tenths. The number with 7 tenths is greater.

146.079 is less than 146.792. Using inequality symbols, this becomes $146.079 < 146.792$.

EXAMPLE

Compare the decimals 274.061 and 274.601 using the symbols >, <, or =.

$274.061 < 274.601$

When comparing decimal values, compare each digit from left to right. When comparing 274.061 and 274.601, start by comparing the value in the hundreds place. Both values have a 2. Move one place value to the right. Both values have a 7. Move one place value to the right. Both values have a 4. Move one place value to the right. 274.061 has a 0 in the tenths place, and 274.601 has a 6 in the tenths place. Since $0 < 6$, 274.601 is the larger number.

EXAMPLE

Compare the decimals 57.1 and 57.09 using the symbols >, <, or =.

Answer: $57.1 > 57.09$

Decimals can be compared using place value. Start by comparing the farthest left digit. Both values have a 5 in the tens place. Move one place value to the right. Both digits have a 7 in the ones place. Move one place value to the right. 57.1 has a 1 in the tenths place, and 57.09 has a 0 in the tenths place. Since $1 > 0$, 57.1 is larger than 57.09.

Rounding Decimals

Decimal values fall **between two whole numbers** on a **number line**. For example, 5.7 falls between 5 and 6 on a number line. When rounding a decimal to a whole number, look for the whole number it is closest to on the number line. 5.7 is closer to 6 than 5, so 5.7 rounds to 6. Decimals will not always need to be rounded to the nearest whole number. Decimals can also be rounded to the nearest tenth or hundredth.

For example, round 47.28 to the nearest tenth.

First locate the digit that is in the tenths place. This is 2. Now look to the digit to the right. In this case, the number is 8. If this digit is 5 or more, then the tenths digit will round up. If this digit is 4 or less, the tenths digit will remain the same.

2 is in the tenths place, and 8 is to the right. This means the 2 will round up to 3, so 47.28 rounds to 47.3. This also means that 47.28 is closer to 47.3 than 47.2 on a number line.

The same process applies when rounding numbers to the hundredths place.

For example, round 309.274 to the nearest hundredth.

First locate the digit in the hundredths place. This is 7. Now look to the digit to the right. In this case, the number is 4. Since this digit is 4 or less, the digit in the hundredths place will remain the same. 309.274 rounds to 309.27. This also means that 309.274 is closer to 309.27 than 309.28 on a number line.

Review Video: Rounding and Estimation
Visit mometrix.com/academy and enter code: 126243

Estimating

Many addition, subtraction, multiplication, and division word problems can be solved using estimation. **Estimation** means calculating an **approximate** answer. Estimation can also be used as a strategy for checking the accuracy or reasonableness of an answer. For example, if the estimated amount of time it took you to run 3 miles was 30 minutes, but your calculation showed 300 minutes, you would know that there was an error in your math. Fluency, mental math, and strategies such as compatible numbers can make estimation a quick process. The goal is to use estimation as a quick reference point for the accuracy of an answer. For example, consider the following example:

Hank pays \$231 for groceries. Betty pays \$198 for groceries. About how much more did Hank pay than Betty?

Use estimation to solve. The question asks "about" how much more, which indicates that estimation will be sufficient. Consider rounding each number to the nearest ten. \$231 becomes \$230, and \$198 becomes \$200. The difference between \$230 and \$200 can be calculated mentally, $\$230 - \$200 = \$30$. Hank spent about \$30 more than Betty.

Estimation strategies can also be used for multiplication and division scenarios:

Paul bought one large bag of dog food. The bag weighs 48 pounds. If Paul feeds his dog 5 cups of food each day, about how many days will the dog food last?

Use estimation to solve. The problem asks "about" how many days, which indicates that estimation is sufficient. The 48-pound bag needs to be divided into groups of 5 to calculate the number of days. However, 48 is not divisible by 5. 48 is close to 50, and 50 is divisible by 5, $50 \div 5 = 10$. So, the bag of dog food will last about 10 days.

Multiplying Multi-Digit Numbers

There are many ways to multiply multi-digit numbers. Some strategies include partial products, the distributive property, the lattice method, and the standard algorithm. The **standard algorithm** is a popular strategy because it is time effective. This process multiplies each digit in one number by each digit in the other number, based on place value. Start by lining up the ones digit for both numbers and stack the two numbers vertically with the larger number on top. For example, when multiplying 526×31, line up the ones digits, and stack the numbers with 526 on top.

$$\begin{array}{r} 526 \\ \times\ 31 \\ \hline \end{array}$$

Step 1: Multiply the 1 by all digits in 526. This is similar to the distributive property. The result is 526.

$$\begin{array}{r} 526 \\ \times \quad 31 \\ \hline 526 \end{array}$$

Step 2: Write a "place holder zero" under the 6, and cross out the 1. The ones digit has been distributed, and the tens digit is next. The place holder zero will keep the columns aligned during the next round of multiplication.

$$\begin{array}{r} 526 \\ \times \quad 3\not{1} \\ \hline 526 \\ 0 \end{array}$$

Step 3: Multiply the 3 by all digits in 526. Consider drawing loops over each digit to stay organized. $3 \times 6 = 18$. Notice how 18 is split up into ones and tens. The 1 is placed over tens column, and the 8 is placed under the answer line in the tens column.

$$\begin{array}{r} 1 \\ 526 \\ \times \quad 3\not{1} \\ \hline 526 \\ 80 \end{array}$$

Step 4: Move to the next digit: $3 \times 2 = 6$. Add the 1 (above). $6 + 1 = 7$, so write 7 under the answer line in the next spot (hundreds place).

$$\begin{array}{r} 1 \\ 526 \\ \times \quad 3\not{1} \\ \hline 526 \\ 80 \end{array}$$

Step 5: Move to the last digit: $3 \times 5 = 15$. Write 15 under the answer line in the ten thousands and thousands place.

```
      1
    526
  ×  31
  -----
    526
+ 15780
-------
```

Step 6: Use the standard algorithm to find the sum of the two rows of numbers under the answer line. The sum of 526 and 15,780 is 16,306. This means that the product of 526 and 31 is 16,306.

```
      1
    526
  ×  31
  -----
    ¹526
   ₁
+ 15780
-------
 16,306
```

Dividing Multi-Digit Numbers

The standard algorithm for multi-digit division is commonly referred to as **long division**. In this strategy, the **dividend** is placed under the division symbol, and the **divisor** is placed to the left of the division symbol. The answer will be placed above the symbol, and the work will occur under the symbol. For example, when dividing 3,190 by 58, place 3,190 under the symbol and 58 to the left of the symbol.

3,190 ÷ 58 becomes:

```
   ____
58)3190
```

The standard algorithm follows a 4-step process.

Step 1: Divide
Step 2: Multiply
Step 3: Subtract
Step 4: Bring Down

Step 1: Figure out how many times the divisor can fit into the first digit of the dividend without going over it. In this case, 58 cannot go into 3 because 3 is too small. Include the next digit. Again, 58 cannot go into 31 because 31 is too small. Include the next digit. 58 can go into 319 because 319 is larger than 58. Use estimation to determine how many times 58 goes into 319. Round 58 to 60. Round 319 to 300. 60 goes into 300 5 times. This estimation can be used to determine how many times 58 goes into 319. Write 5 above the 9. Make sure the 5 is above the hundreds digit because this is the farthest place value considered in the estimation.

```
     5
   ____
```

$$58\overline{)3190}$$

Step 2: Multiply 5 × 58. The product of 5 × 58 is 290. Write 290 below the dividend.

$$\begin{array}{r} 5 \\ 58\overline{)3190} \\ 290 \end{array}$$

Step 3: Subtract 319 − 290 = 29.

$$\begin{array}{r} 5 \\ 58\overline{)3190} \\ \underline{-290} \\ 29 \end{array}$$

Step 4: Bring down the next digit and repeat the process.

$$\begin{array}{r} 55 \\ 58\overline{)3190} \\ \underline{-290} \\ 290 \\ \underline{-290} \\ 0 \end{array}$$

The last value is 0. This indicates that there is no remainder and that 3,190 ÷ 58 = 55.

Representing Decimals with Money

Money is expressed in **dollars** and **cents**. Cents are represented as **tenths** and **hundredths**. For example, $4.92 represents 4 whole dollars, 9 tenths of a dollar, and 2 hundredths of a dollar.

Express the coins as a decimal dollar amount:

4 quarters, 4 nickels, 2 pennies.

4 quarters: $0.25 + $0.25 + $0.25 + $0.25 = $1.00

4 nickels: $0.05 + $0.05 + $0.05 + $0.05 = $0.20

2 pennies: $0.01 + $0.01 = $0.02

Remember, line up the decimal points when adding decimals.

$$\begin{array}{r} 1.\ 00 \\ 0.\ 20 \\ \underline{+0.\ 02} \\ \$1.\ 22 \end{array}$$

EXAMPLE

Consider the model below. What fraction would this represent? What decimal? What dollar amount?

The model shows $\frac{100}{100}+\frac{10}{10}+\frac{23}{100}$.

This represents 2 wholes and 23 hundredths.

As a decimal, this is 2.23.

As a dollar amount, this represents $2.23.

Adding and Subtracting Decimals and Whole Numbers

The important thing to remember when adding and subtracting decimal numbers is to **line up** the **decimal points**. Lining up the decimal points ensures that similar place values are being combined. For example, ones combine with ones, tens combine with tens.

Consider the following: A pizza costs $27.50 and a drink costs $4.65. The total cost of the meal can be calculated by finding the sum. Stack the numbers vertically and line up the decimal points. With addition, it does not matter which number is on top or bottom. Regroup if necessary and bring the decimal straight down into the answer line. This method is known as the **standard algorithm**.

$$\begin{array}{r} 11 \\ 27.50 \\ +\ 4.65 \\ \hline \$32.15 \end{array}$$

The standard algorithm is also useful for subtraction scenarios. For example, if a piece of ribbon measures 132.1 centimeters, and 27.76 centimeters are cut off and removed, how many centimeters of ribbon are left?

Stack the values vertically and line up the decimals. Make sure the larger number, 132.1, is on the top. Sometimes it is helpful to fill in any empty spaces with a zero. Regroup if necessary, and again bring the decimal straight down into the answer line.

$$\begin{array}{rrrcrr} & & 11 & & 10 & \\ & 2 & \cancel{1} & & \cancel{0} & 10 \\ 1 & \cancel{3} & \cancel{2} & . & \cancel{1} & \cancel{0} \\ - & 2 & 7 & . & 7 & 6 \\ \hline 1 & 0 & 4 & . & 3 & 4 \end{array}$$

There are 104.34 centimeters of ribbon left.

Review Video: Adding and Subtracting Decimals
Visit mometrix.com/academy and enter code: 381101

EXAMPLE

Solve using the standard algorithm: $40.03 - 26.12 =$ ____

Line up the decimals when adding and subtracting decimals. Regrouping is required for this problem.

$$\begin{array}{r} \overset{3}{\cancel{4}}\overset{\overset{9}{\cancel{10}}}{\cancel{0}}.\overset{10}{\cancel{0}}3 \\ -26.12 \\ \hline 13.91 \end{array}$$

$$40.03 - 26.12 = 13.91$$

Check for accuracy using addition: $13.91 + 26.12 = 40.03$.

EXAMPLE

Solve using the standard algorithm: $63.04 + 99.09 =$ ____.

$$\begin{array}{r} \overset{1}{6}3.\overset{1}{0}4 \\ +99.09 \\ \hline 162.13 \end{array}$$

Line up the decimals when adding and subtracting decimals: $63.04 + 99.09 = 162.13$.

Representing the Multiplication of Decimals

When multiplying decimals, consider using modeling strategies such as an **area model**. For example, when multiplying 0.6×0.7, use a hundreds grid. Start by shading in 6 tenths vertically.

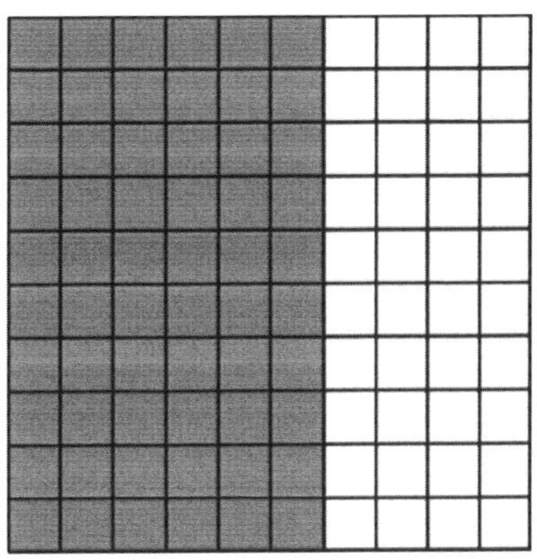

Now shade in 7 tenths horizontally. Notice how one region of the hundreds grid has shading that is now overlapping.

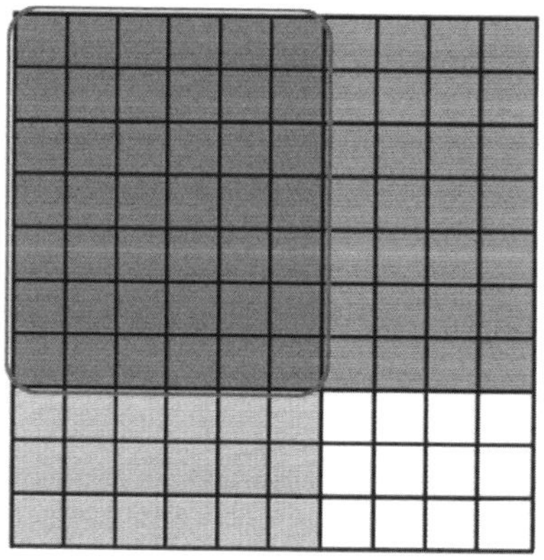

There are 42 hundredths that are shaded and overlapping. This means that the product of 0.6 and 0.7 is 0.42.

When multiplying a decimal by a decimal, consider setting up a slightly different area model. For example, when multiplying 2.3×1.4, start by setting up a square with 4 equal sections. Now write 2.3 as 2 and 0.3, and 1.4 as 1 and 0.4. Fill in the 4 empty squares with the products of each pair. For example, $1 \times 2 = 2$, $1 \times 0.3 = 0.3$, $0.4 \times 2 = 0.8$, and $0.4 \times 0.3 = 0.12$. Now find the sum of all four values: $2 + 0.3 + 0.8 + 0.12 = 3.22$. This means that the product of 2.3 and 1.4 is 3.22.

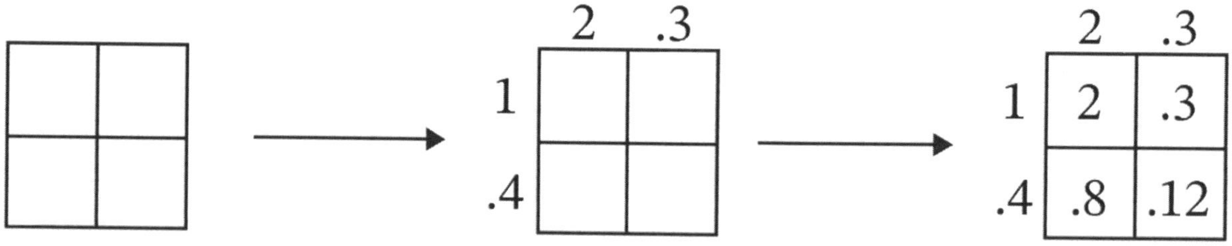

Strategies for Multiplying Decimals

Decimals can be multiplied using strategies involving **place value** or the **standard algorithm**. For example, when a decimal is multiplied by a power of 10, the decimal moves one place to the right. When a decimal is divided by a power of 10, the decimal moves one place to the left. This can be applied to situations involving money.

For example:

$\$4.55 \times 10 = \$45.50$
$\$4.55 \times 100 = \$455.00$
$\$45.50 \div 10 = \$4.55$
$\$455.00 \div 100 = \$4.55$

When decimals are multiplied by whole numbers that are not powers of 10, the standard algorithm can be used. Start by stacking the longer number on top of the smaller number. Shift the numbers to the right. There is no need to line up the decimals. For example, 2.74 × 6.1 becomes:

$$\begin{array}{r} 2.74 \\ \underline{\times\ 6.1} \end{array}$$

Multiply the 1 by each digit in 2.74.
Add a place holder 0.
Multiply the 6 by each digit in 2.74
Find the sum.

Place the decimal. Count the total number of digits to the right of the decimal in 2.74 and 6.1 In this case, there is a total of 3 digits to the right of the decimal. Move the decimal 3 places to the left so that 16714 becomes 16.714. The product of 2.74 and 6.1 is 16.714.

$$\begin{array}{r} {}^{4}\ \ {}^{2}\ \ \ \\ 2.7\,4 \\ \underline{\times\ \ 6.1} \\ 2{}^{1}7\,4 \\ \underline{+\ 16\,4\,4\,0} \\ \boxed{16.7\,1\,4} \end{array}$$

EXAMPLE

A shop owner chargers $8.50 for homemade candles. What is the cost a customer pays for purchasing 10 candles?

$85.00

When a number is multiplied by 10, the decimal point moves one place to the right. This is true when multiplying decimal dollar amounts such as $8.50 × 10. The decimal in $8.50 moves one place to the right, and the product becomes $85.00.

EXAMPLE

A baker needs apples for an apple strudel recipe. The baker uses 4 apples that each weigh 3.5 ounces. How many ounces of apples were used?

14 ounces

The baker uses 4 apples that each weigh 3.5 ounces. This means there are 4 groups of 3.5. Multiplication can be used to determine the total number of ounces. Consider using partial products. 4 × 3.5 can be thought of as (4 × 3) + (4 × 0.5). 4 groups of 3 is 12, and 4 groups of 0.5 is 2. Then, 12 + 2 = 14. So, the baker used 14 ounces of apples for the strudel.

Representing the Division of Decimals

Long division is not the only way to divide numbers with decimals. Decimals can be divided using objects, pictorial models, and area models. For example, consider the following scenario: 1.92 pounds of lemon juice are poured into 12 small containers. How many pounds of lemon juice will be in each container? This scenario represents a division problem: $1.92 \div 12$. 1.92 is the same thing as 192 hundredths. Draw a box to represent 192 hundredths divided by 12.

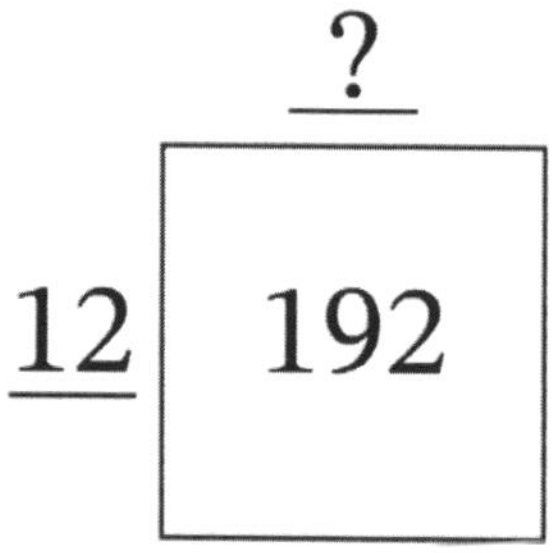

About how many times does 12 fit into 192, without going over? Select a number that is easy to work with without a calculator. For example, choose 10. Write 10 on the answer line, and write the product of 12×10 in the box. Subtract to calculate the leftover amount.

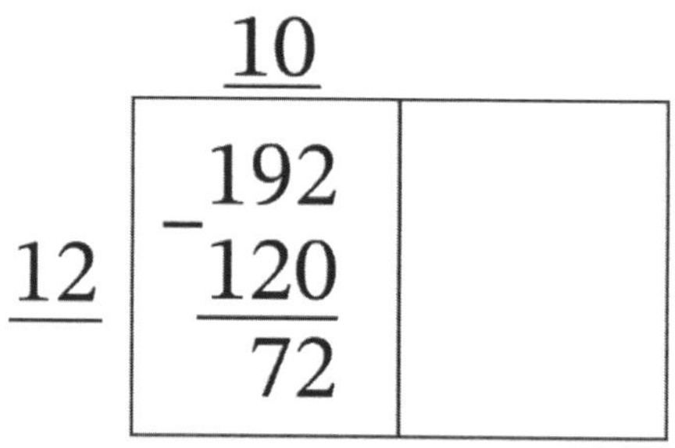

The leftover amount is 72. Set up another box and another answer line. Repeat the process. How many times does 12 fit into 72, without going over? The answer is 6. Write 6 on the answer line. Subtract to find the leftover amount.

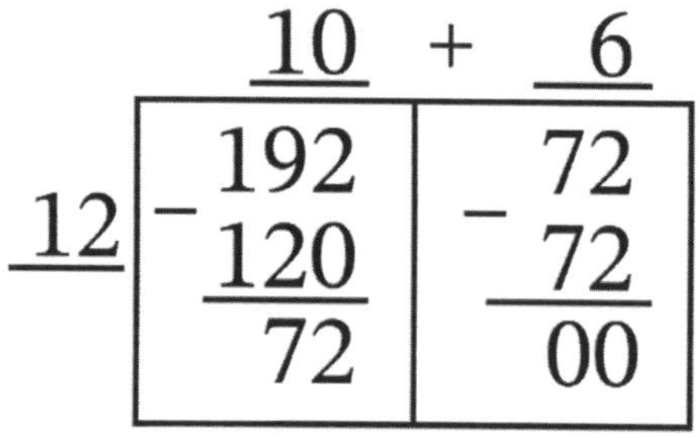

Find the sum: $10 + 6 = 16$. Remember, 16 represents 16 hundredths. This means that the quotient of 1.92 and 12 is 0.16.

Strategies for Dividing Decimals

The standard algorithm, commonly known as long division, can be used to divide decimals. For example, consider the division problem $65.35 \div 2.5$. The first thing to notice is that there is a decimal in the divisor. This needs to be adjusted. The divisor cannot contain a decimal. Get rid of this by multiplying both values by 10. 2.5 becomes 25, and 65.35 becomes 653.5. Now the problem can continue. Remember the 4-step process for long division.

Step 1: Divide
Step 2: Multiply
Step 3: Subtract
Step 4: Bring Down

Bring the decimal straight up into the answer line. The result is 26.14.

```
      26.14
25) 653.50
   -50
    153
   -150
      35
     -25
     100
    -100
       0
```

EXAMPLE

Jon spent $362.50 on 10 sweaters. Each sweater was the same price. What was the cost of each sweater?

$36.25

When a decimal value is divided by 10, the decimal point moves one place to the left. This process applies to decimal dollar amounts. $362.50 divided by 10 becomes $36.25.

EXAMPLE

A coach pours 28.4 gallons of sports drink into 8 containers. How many gallons of sports drink will be in each container?

3.55 gallons

Since we are dividing a whole into different parts, we will use division. Consider using the standard algorithm for long division. Follow the four-step process for long division: Divide, Multiply, Subtract, Bring Down. Then repeat. The result is 3.55 gallons.

```
    3.55
8) 28.40
  -24
    44
   -40
     40
    -40
      0
```

Adding and Subtracting Rational Numbers

It is important to feel comfortable adding and subtracting numbers fluently. Consider using strategies involving place value or estimation when adding and subtracting. For example, if a savings account contains $4,680 and a checking account contains $2,315 and you need to calculate the total of both accounts combined, place value can be helpful. Add the digits in the corresponding place values to calculate the sum mentally. There are 4 + 2 thousands, 6 + 3 hundreds, 8 + 1 tens, and 0 + 5 ones. This means there is a total of $6,995 in both accounts.

Consider **estimation strategies** to calculate the difference between dollar amounts in each account. The savings account contains $4,680 which rounds to $4,700 when rounded to the nearest hundred. The checking account contains $2,300 when rounded to the nearest hundred. Subtract these values mentally to get an approximate answer: $4,700 − $2,300 = $2,400. This means that the savings account has approximately $2,400 more than the checking account.

Example

Julia purchases a backpack for $31, a notebook for $5.50, and a pack of pencils for $9.50. Julia has $55 in cash. Does she have enough money to buy all three items?

Yes, she has enough money to buy all three items.

Start by finding the total cost of the 3 items. Consider using compatible numbers. $31 and $9 combine to $40. Now add $5 for the notebook. The total is now $45. Now add the cents. $45 + $0.50 + $0.50 = $46. The total is $46. Julia has $55 in cash, so she has enough money to purchase all three items.

Example

A small backyard swimming pool contains 3,398 gallons of water. A pool cleaning company is draining the pool to clean the interior of the pool. At noon the pool contains 2,129 gallons of water. How many gallons of water has been drained from the pool so far?

1,269 gallons

The pool started with 3,398 gallons of water and at noon contains 2,129 gallons. Subtract to determine the number of gallons that have been drained. Use the standard algorithm, and stack 3,398 over 2,129 so that the place value is lined up. Subtract columns from right to left. Regroup if necessary: 3,398 − 2,129 = 1,269.

$$\begin{array}{r} 1 \\ 88 \\ 33\not{9}\not{8} \\ -2129 \\ \hline 1269 \end{array}$$

The pool has drained 1,269 gallons of water by noon.

Numbers and Operations – Fractions

Fractions

A **fraction** is a number that is expressed as one integer written above another integer, with a dividing line between them $\left(\frac{x}{y}\right)$. It represents the **quotient** of the two numbers "x divided by y." It can also be thought of as x out of y equal parts.

The top number of a fraction is called the **numerator**, and it represents the number of parts under consideration. The 1 in $\frac{1}{4}$ means that 1 part out of the whole is being considered in the calculation. The bottom number of a fraction is called the **denominator**, and it represents the total number of equal parts. The 4 in $\frac{1}{4}$ means that the whole consists of 4 equal parts. A fraction cannot have a denominator of zero; this is referred to as "*undefined*."

Fractions can be manipulated, without changing the value of the fraction, by multiplying or dividing (but not adding or subtracting) both the numerator and denominator by the same number. If you divide both numbers by a common factor, you are **reducing** or simplifying the fraction. Two fractions that have the same value but are expressed differently are known as **equivalent fractions**. For example, $\frac{2}{10}, \frac{3}{15}, \frac{4}{20}$, and $\frac{5}{25}$ are all equivalent fractions. They can also all be reduced or simplified to $\frac{1}{5}$.

When two fractions are manipulated so that they have the same denominator, this is known as finding a **common denominator**. The number chosen to be that common denominator should be the least common multiple of the two original denominators. Example: $\frac{3}{4}$ and $\frac{5}{6}$; the least common multiple of 4 and 6 is 12. Manipulating to achieve the common denominator: $\frac{3}{4} = \frac{9}{12}; \frac{5}{6} = \frac{10}{12}$.

Review Video: Overview of Fractions
Visit mometrix.com/academy and enter code: 262335

Proper Fractions and Mixed Numbers

A fraction whose denominator is greater than its numerator is known as a **proper fraction**, while a fraction whose numerator is greater than its denominator is known as an **improper fraction**. Proper fractions have values *less than one* and improper fractions have values *greater than one.*

A **mixed number** is a number that contains both an integer and a fraction. Any improper fraction can be rewritten as a mixed number. Example: $\frac{8}{3} = \frac{6}{3} + \frac{2}{3} = 2 + \frac{2}{3} = 2\frac{2}{3}$. Similarly, any mixed number can be rewritten as an improper fraction. Example: $1\frac{3}{5} = 1 + \frac{3}{5} = \frac{5}{5} + \frac{3}{5} = \frac{8}{5}$.

Review Video: Proper and Improper Fractions and Mixed Numbers
Visit mometrix.com/academy and enter code: 211077

ADDING AND SUBTRACTING FRACTIONS

If two fractions have a common denominator, they can be added or subtracted simply by adding or subtracting the two numerators and retaining the same denominator. If the two fractions do not already have the same denominator, one or both of them must be manipulated to achieve a common denominator before they can be added or subtracted. Example: $\frac{1}{2}+\frac{1}{4}=\frac{2}{4}+\frac{1}{4}=\frac{3}{4}$.

Review Video: Adding and Subtracting Fractions
Visit mometrix.com/academy and enter code: 378080

MULTIPLYING FRACTIONS

Two fractions can be multiplied by multiplying the two numerators to find the new numerator and the two denominators to find the new denominator. Example: $\frac{1}{3}\times\frac{2}{3}=\frac{1\times2}{3\times3}=\frac{2}{9}$.

DIVIDING FRACTIONS

Two fractions can be divided by flipping the numerator and denominator of the second fraction and then proceeding as though it were a multiplication problem. Example: $\frac{2}{3}\div\frac{3}{4}=\frac{2}{3}\times\frac{4}{3}=\frac{8}{9}$.

Review Video: Multiplying and Dividing Fractions
Visit mometrix.com/academy and enter code: 473632

Solving Problems Involving Fractions

ADDING AND SUBTRACTING FRACTIONS

Fractions can be added or subtracted using objects or models. For example, to solve the problem $\frac{1}{2}+\frac{2}{10}$, draw a rectangle with 10 equal parts. Shade $\frac{1}{2}$ of the rectangle, then shade $\frac{2}{10}$ of the rectangle. The sum is the total amount of the rectangle that has been shaded. In this case, $\frac{7}{10}$. The sum of $\frac{1}{2}$ and $\frac{2}{10}$ is $\frac{7}{10}$.

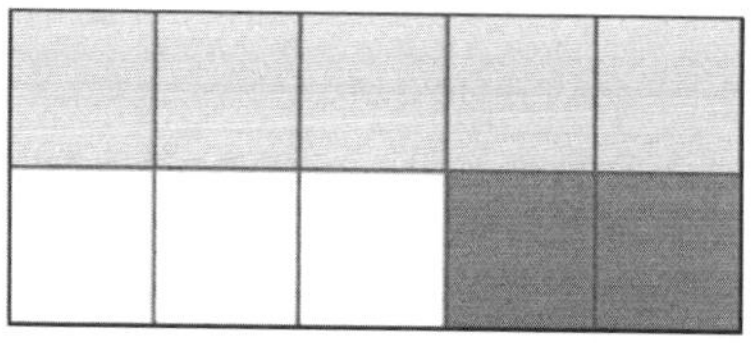

A similar modeling concept can be used when subtracting fractions. Consider the problem $\frac{1}{2}-\frac{3}{8}$. The fractions have different denominators, but a model can still be helpful. Shade half of the rectangle, this shaded region represents $\frac{1}{2}$. To subtract $\frac{3}{8}$ from this, start by dividing the whole into eighths.

Now cross off 3 of those eighths. Now there is only one shaded eighth remaining. This means $\frac{1}{2} - \frac{3}{8} = \frac{1}{8}$.

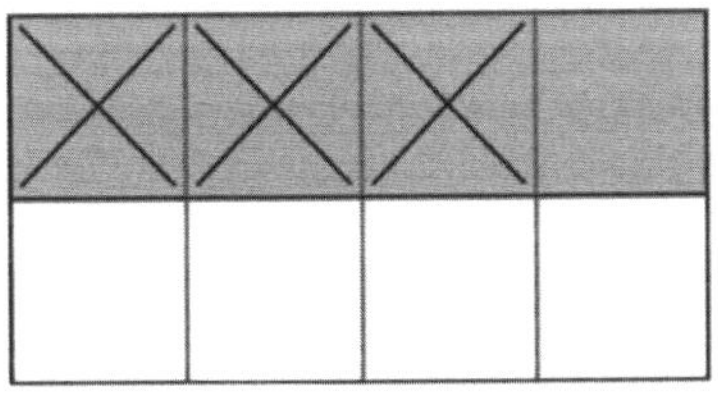

Review Video: Adding and Subtracting Fractions
Visit mometrix.com/academy and enter code: 378080

MULTIPLYING FRACTIONS AND WHOLE NUMBERS

Modeling strategies can be helpful when multiplying a whole number by a fraction. For example, $4 \times \frac{2}{3}$ can be thought of as 4 groups of $\frac{2}{3}$. There are 8 thirds altogether, so $4 \times \frac{2}{3} = \frac{8}{3}$, or as a mixed number, $2\frac{2}{3}$.

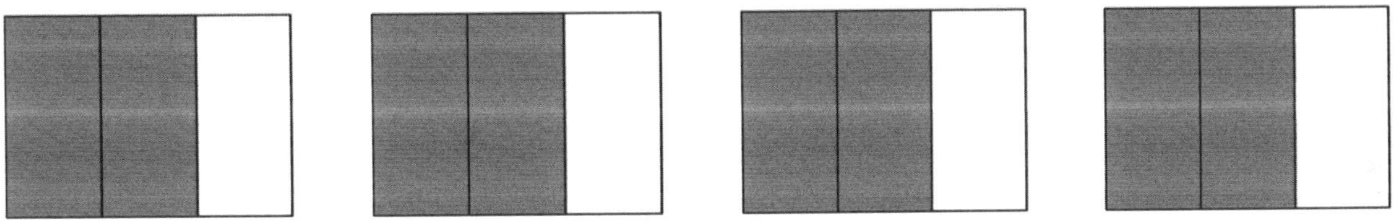

Multiplication is commutative, meaning the order does not matter. This same modeling strategy applies in situations where the fraction is listed first and the whole number is listed second.

MULTIPLYING A MIXED NUMBER BY A WHOLE NUMBER OR A DECIMAL

When multiplying a mixed number by something, it is usually best to convert it to an improper fraction first. Additionally, if the multiplicand is a decimal, it is most often simplest to convert it to a fraction. For instance, to multiply $4\frac{3}{8}$ by 3.5, begin by rewriting each quantity as a whole number plus a proper fraction. Remember, a mixed number is a fraction added to a whole number and a decimal is a representation of the sum of fractions, specifically tenths, hundredths, thousandths, and so on:

$$4\frac{3}{8} \times 3.5 = \left(4 + \frac{3}{8}\right) \times \left(3 + \frac{1}{2}\right)$$

Next, the quantities being added need to be expressed with the same denominator. This is achieved by multiplying and dividing the whole number by the denominator of the fraction. Recall that a whole number is equivalent to that number divided by 1:

$$= \left(\frac{4}{1} \times \frac{8}{8} + \frac{3}{8}\right) \times \left(\frac{3}{1} \times \frac{2}{2} + \frac{1}{2}\right)$$

When multiplying fractions, remember to multiply the numerators and denominators separately:

$$= \left(\frac{4 \times 8}{1 \times 8} + \frac{3}{8}\right) \times \left(\frac{3 \times 2}{1 \times 2} + \frac{1}{2}\right)$$
$$= \left(\frac{32}{8} + \frac{3}{8}\right) \times \left(\frac{6}{2} + \frac{1}{2}\right)$$

Now that the fractions have the same denominators, they can be added:

$$= \frac{35}{8} \times \frac{7}{2}$$

Finally, perform the last multiplication and then simplify:

$$= \frac{35 \times 7}{8 \times 2} = \frac{245}{16} = \frac{240}{16} + \frac{5}{16} = 15\frac{5}{16}$$

Dividing Fractions and Whole Numbers

One way to visualize the concept of fraction division is to use a model. For example, when dividing a unit fraction by a whole number, start by drawing a model of the fraction. For example, for the problem $\frac{1}{8} \div 3$, start by modeling eighths, and then shade one share.

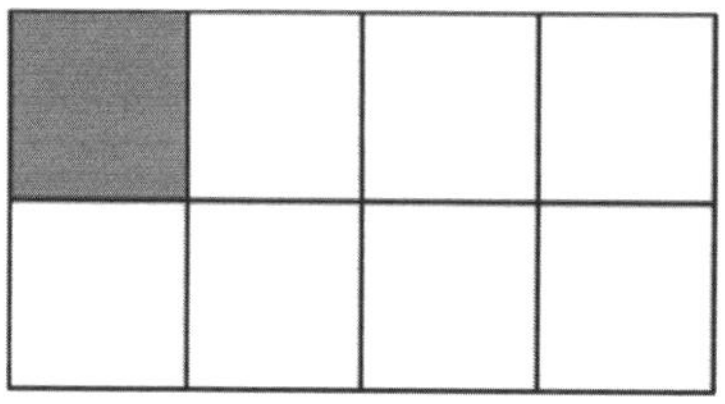

Now divide this shaded eighth into 3 equal shares. The size of one of these shares is now $\frac{1}{24}$ because dividing each eighth into 3 gives 24 total shares. This means that $\frac{1}{8} \div 3 = \frac{1}{24}$.

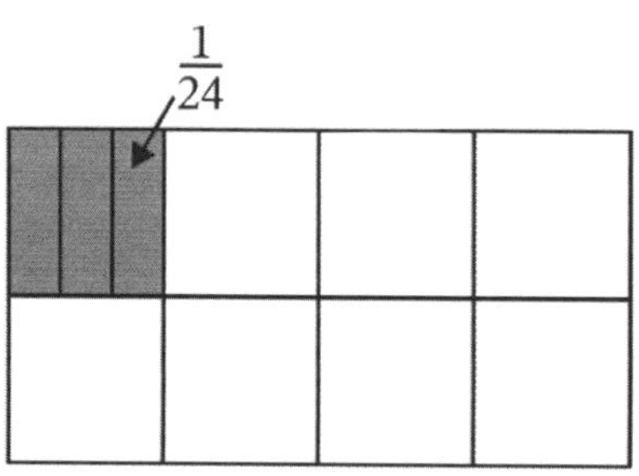

A similar process works when dividing a whole number by a unit fraction. For example,

Consider $4 \div \frac{1}{5}$. Start by drawing a model for 4. Then divide each whole into fifths. How many fifths are there altogether? In this case, there are 20. This means that $4 \div \frac{1}{5}$ is equal to 20.

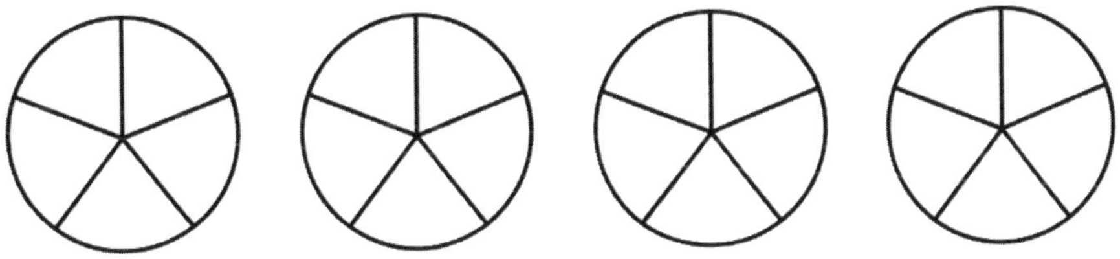

Using Models when Dividing Fractions and Whole Numbers

Consider using a model when dividing fractions by whole numbers or whole numbers by fractions. For example, when calculating $\frac{1}{4} \div 3$, start by modeling $\frac{1}{4}$.

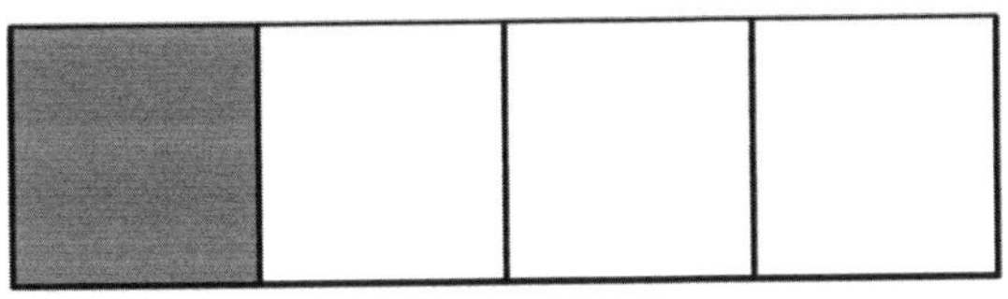

Now divide $\frac{1}{4}$ into 3 equal shares.

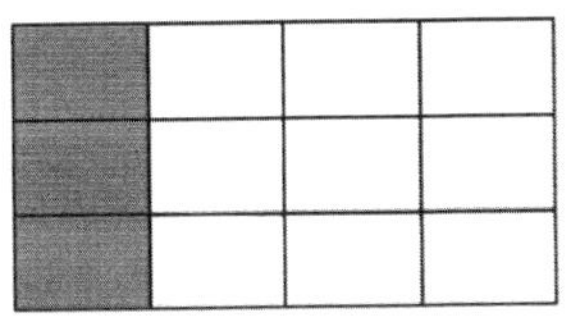

The size of one share is $\frac{1}{12}$. This means that $\frac{1}{4} \div 3$ is $\frac{1}{12}$.

When dividing a whole number by a fraction, use a similar approach. For example, to divide 5 by $\frac{1}{2}$, start by modeling 5 wholes.

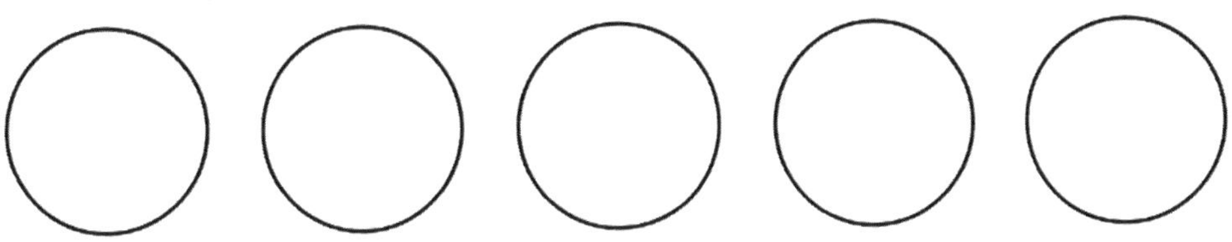

Now divide each whole into halves.

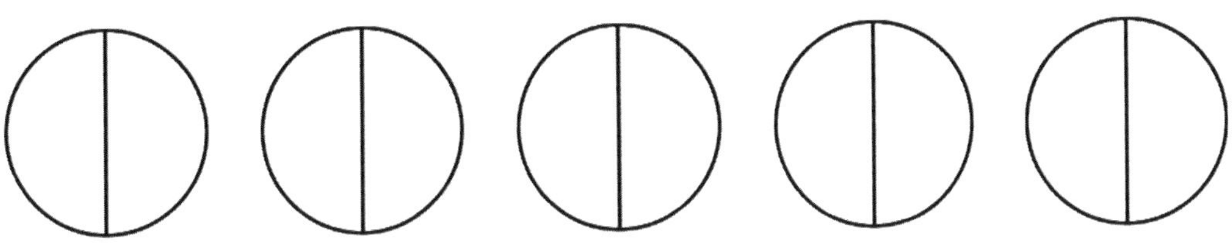

There are 10 halves. This means that $5 \div \frac{1}{2} = 10$.

Another strategy used for dividing whole numbers and fractions involves two steps:
The steps can be referred to as "Multiply and Flip."

For example, to calculate $6 \div \frac{1}{5}$, use the Multiply and Flip technique.

Change the division symbol to a multiplication symbol and flip the second fraction.

6 can be written as $\frac{6}{1}$. $\frac{6}{1} \div \frac{1}{5}$ becomes $\frac{6}{1} \times \frac{5}{1}$. Now multiply the numerators and multiply the denominators. $\frac{6}{1} \times \frac{5}{1}$ becomes $\frac{30}{1}$, or 30.

Example

A chef is making pizzas. The chef has 12 pounds of dough, and each crust requires $\frac{1}{7}$ pound of dough. How many pizza crusts can the chef make?

84 pizza crusts

There are 12 pounds of dough, and it needs to be divided into groups of $\frac{1}{7}$. To divide 12 by $\frac{1}{7}$, start by writing both values in fraction form. $12 \div \frac{1}{7}$ becomes $\frac{12}{1} \div \frac{1}{7}$. Now, follow the "flip and multiply" strategy. Change the division symbol to multiplication, and then flip the second fraction. $\frac{12}{1} \div \frac{1}{7}$ becomes $\frac{12}{1} \times \frac{7}{1}$. Now, multiply across and simplify if possible. $\frac{12}{1} \times \frac{7}{1}$ becomes $\frac{84}{1}$, or 84. The chef can make 84 pizza crusts.

Example

Matt has $\frac{1}{4}$ of his birthday cake left over. Matt and two of his friends want to share the leftover cake. If he divides the leftover cake into 3 equal shares, what fraction of a whole cake will each person receive?

$$\frac{1}{12}$$

The scenario can be represented as a division problem. $\frac{1}{4}$ of the cake is being divided into 3 shares is $\frac{1}{4} \div 3$. To divide fractions and whole numbers, set up both values as a fraction. $\frac{1}{4} \div 3$ becomes $\frac{1}{4} \div \frac{3}{1}$. Follow the "flip and multiply" technique. Change the division symbol to multiplication and flip the second fraction. $\frac{1}{4} \div \frac{3}{1}$ becomes $\frac{1}{4} \times \frac{1}{3}$. Now, multiply straight across and simplify if possible, $\frac{1}{4} \times \frac{1}{3} = \frac{1}{12}$. So, each person will receive $\frac{1}{12}$ of the original whole cake.

Division Displayed as a Fraction

Division is a common operation that can be represented in many ways. For example, division can be expressed through language and symbols. Division can also be expressed as a fraction. For example, $\frac{20}{5}$ is another way of writing 20 divided by 5 or $20 \div 5$. It is important to note that the numerator will always be divided by the denominator. Therefore, the numerator is the **dividend**, and the denominator is the **divisor**. This is still true for fractional values where the value in the numerator is less than the value in the denominator. For example, $\frac{2}{7}$ is another way of writing 2 divided by 7 or $2 \div 7$. When performing this operation, a decimal value will be created.

Comparing Fractions

It is important to master the ability to compare and order fractions. This skill is relevant to many real-world scenarios. For example, carpenters often compare fractional construction nail lengths when preparing for a project, and bakers often compare fractional measurements to have the correct ratio of ingredients. There are three commonly used strategies when comparing fractions. These strategies are referred to as the common denominator approach, the decimal approach, and the cross-multiplication approach.

Using a Common Denominator to Compare Fractions

The fractions $\frac{2}{3}$ and $\frac{4}{7}$ have different denominators. $\frac{2}{3}$ has a denominator of 3, and $\frac{4}{7}$ has a denominator of 7. In order to precisely compare these two fractions, it is necessary to use a common denominator. A common denominator is a common multiple that is shared by both denominators. In this case, the denominators 3 and 7 share a multiple of 21. In general, it is most efficient to select the least common multiple for the two denominators.

Rewrite each fraction with the common denominator of 21. Then, calculate the new numerators as illustrated below.

$$\frac{2}{3} \overset{\times 7}{=} \frac{14}{21} \qquad \frac{4}{7} \overset{\times 3}{=} \frac{12}{21}$$

For $\frac{2}{3}$, multiply the numerator and denominator by 7. The result is $\frac{14}{21}$.

For $\frac{4}{7}$, multiply the numerator and denominator by 3. The result is $\frac{12}{21}$.

Now that both fractions have a denominator of 21, the fractions can accurately be compared by comparing the numerators. Since 14 is greater than 12, the fraction $\frac{14}{21}$ is greater than $\frac{12}{21}$. This means that $\frac{2}{3}$ is greater than $\frac{4}{7}$.

Using Decimals to Compare Fractions

Sometimes decimal values are easier to compare than fraction values. For example, $\frac{5}{8}$ is equivalent to 0.625 and $\frac{3}{5}$ is equivalent to 0.6. This means that the comparison of $\frac{5}{8}$ and $\frac{3}{5}$ can be determined by comparing the decimals 0.625 and 0.6. When both decimal values are extended to the thousandths place, they become 0.625 and 0.600, respectively. It becomes clear that 0.625 is greater than 0.600 because 625 thousandths is greater than 600 thousandths. In other words, $\frac{5}{8}$ is greater than $\frac{3}{5}$ because 0.625 is greater than 0.6.

Using Cross-Multiplication to Compare Fractions

Cross-multiplication is an efficient strategy for comparing fractions. This is a shortcut for the common denominator strategy. Start by writing each fraction next to one another. Multiply the numerator of the fraction on the left by the denominator of the fraction on the right. Write down the result next to the fraction on the left. Now multiply the numerator of the fraction on the right by the denominator of the fraction on the left. Write down the result next to the fraction on the right. Compare both products. The fraction with the larger result is the larger fraction.

Consider the fractions $\frac{4}{7}$ and $\frac{5}{9}$.

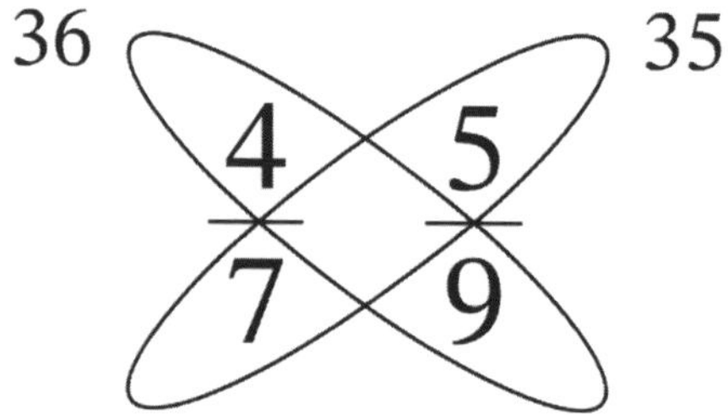

36 is greater than 35. Therefore, $\frac{4}{7}$ is greater than $\frac{5}{9}$.

Measurements and Data

Calculating Conversions

Volume, distance, and mass can be measured using the metric system or the customary system. The **metric system** is generally preferred in math and science because values can be easily multiplied or divided by powers of 10. The metric system is convenient when working with very large or very small values. For example, there are 1,000 meters in one kilometer, so the number of meters can easily be determined if the number of kilometers are provided. For example, there are 5,000 meters in 5 kilometers. 3,000 meters in 3 kilometers. 8,000 meters in 8 kilometers. Metric conversion tables can be helpful for seeing the patterns within the metric system. The table below focuses on the base unit of meters. Notice how 1 meter is equivalent to 1,000 mm, 100 cm, and 0.001 km.

Millimeters	Centimeters	Meters	Kilometers
mm	cm	m	km
1	0.1	0.001	0.000001
10	1	0.01	0.00001
1,000	**100**	**1**	**0.001**
1,000,000	10,000	1,000	1

Review Video: Metric System Conversions
Visit mometrix.com/academy and enter code: 163709

The **customary system** is commonly used in the United States but very rarely in other regions of the world. The units of the customary system are not based on powers of ten. The conversion factors do not follow a pattern, which makes them a bit more challenging to remember. For example, study the table below. Notice how there is not one single pattern or relationship used consistently throughout the table. Each conversion factor is unique to each specific unit. This lack of a consistency is the most significant difference between the metric system and the customary system.

Common Customary Measurements

Length	Weight	Time	Capacity
1 foot = 12 inches 1 yard = 36 inches 1 yard = 3 feet 1 mile = 5,280 feet 1 mile = 1,760 yards	1 pound = 16 ounces 1 ton = 2,000 pounds	1 minute = 60 seconds 1 hour = 60 minutes 1 day = 24 hours 1 week = 7 days 1 year = 12 months 1 year = 365 days 1 leap year = 366 days	1 cup = 8 fluid ounces 1 pint = 2 cups 1 quart = 2 pints 1 quart = 4 cups 1 gallon = 4 quarts 1 gallon = 16 cups

Consider this real-world scenario for a metric conversion. Kristen walks 500 meters to work each morning, and then takes the bus home each evening. If she does this 5 days a week, for 4 weeks, how many kilometers has she walked?

Kristen walks 500 meters, 5 times a week. This means that in one week, she walks 2,500 meters. In 2 weeks she walks 5,000 meters. In 3 weeks she walks 7,500 meters. In 4 weeks she walks 10,000 meters. There are 1,000 meters in each kilometer. This means that the number of kilometers will always be 1,000 times less than the number of meters. Therefore, 10,000 meters is 10 kilometers. 10,000 divided by 1,000 is 10. Kristen has walked 10 kilometers in 4 weeks.

Consider a real-world scenario for where a customary conversion is needed. A long jump runway is 147 feet. How many yards is this?

There are 3 feet in 1 yard. This means that the number of feet will always be 3 times larger than the number of yards. Or, in this case, the number of yards will be 3 times smaller than the number of feet. Divide the number of feet by 3 to calculate the number of yards, $147 \div 3 = 49$. So, the runway is 49 yards long.

Review Video: Measurement Conversion
Visit mometrix.com/academy and enter code: 316703

Dot Plots

Dot plots are graphs used to show trends, clusters, or groupings within data. Dot plots show individual data points as dots on a graph. The data points are not connected to form a line. If the data points were connected, this would be considered a line graph. Dot plots are very similar to frequency tables, except each data point is plotted individually so that the frequency is displayed as a "stack of dots" rather than a number or tally mark. For example, the dot plot below shows 5 dots over the 2 mile category, meaning 5 separate bike riders rode 2 miles.

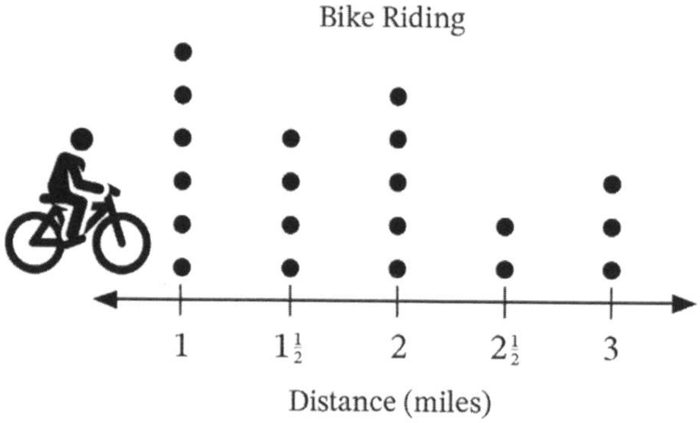

Solving Problems Involving Dot Plots

The display below is a dot plot that represents the weight of backpacks for a group of students. Each dot represents one student. Use the dot plot to answer the following one- and two-step problems.

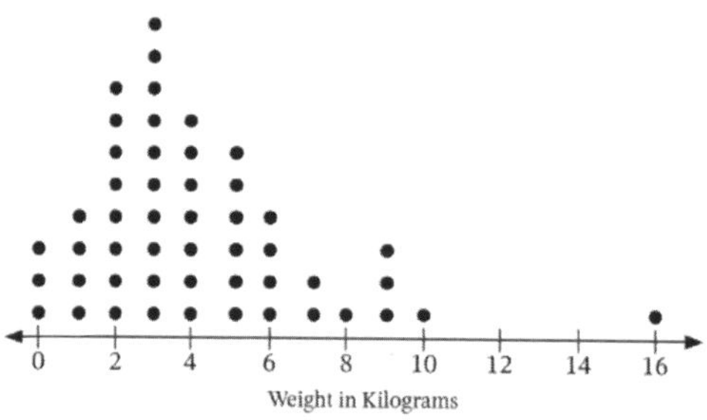

One-Step Problem: How many students are represented on the dot plot?

- Each dot represents 1 student, and there are 50 dots on the dot plot. This means that 50 students are represented on the dot plot.

Two-Step Problem: How many students have a backpack that weighs 6 kilograms or more?

- Identify the weights along the x-axis that are 6 kilograms or more. Weights that are greater than or equal to 6 kilograms include 6 through 16. Count the number of dots located from 6 kilograms to 16 kilograms. In this case, there are 12 dots. Each dot represents 1 student, so 12 students have backpacks that weigh 6 kilograms or more.

Solving Problems Related to Perimeter, Area, and Volume

Many word problems will involve perimeter, area, or volume. **Perimeter** is the distance around a two-dimensional shape. **Area** is the space within a two-dimensional shape. **Volume** is the amount of space within a three-dimensional figure.

For example, consider the following scenario.

A school is installing a new rectangular play field. The field is 200 feet wide and 575 feet long. What is the area of the play field? If a student runs around the perimeter of the play field, how far will he or she run?

Different polygons will have different area formulas. The **area formula for a rectangle** is Area $=$ Length $\times$ Width. Area $=$ Length $\times$ Width becomes $A = 575 \times 200$, which simplifies to 115,000. This means that the total area within the play field is 115,000 square feet.

The perimeter around the play field can be calculated by finding the sum of all four side lengths. In this case, $P = 200 + 200 + 575 + 575$ simplifies to $P = 1{,}550$ feet. If a student runs around the perimeter of the play field, he or she will run 1,550 feet.

Consider another question.

Some of the play field equipment is arriving in large boxes. One piece of equipment arrives in a box that is 14 feet long, 6 feet wide, and 4 feet deep. What is the volume of the equipment box?

Volume formulas will vary depending on the specific three-dimensional figure. In this case, the figure is a rectangular prism. The volume, V, can be calculated as

$V = l \times w \times h$, where l is length, w is width, and h is height or depth. This simplifies to $V = 14 \times 6 \times 4 = 336$, so the volume of the box is 336 cubic feet.

Review Video: Volume and Surface Area of a Cube
Visit mometrix.com/academy and enter code: 664455

Review Video: Volume and Surface Area of a Rectangular Prism
Visit mometrix.com/academy and enter code: 282814

EXAMPLE

A rectangular wooden tabletop is twice as long as it is wide. If the tabletop is 3 feet wide, what is the area of the tabletop?

18 square feet

The area of a rectangle can be calculated using the formula $A = l \times w$, where l and w represent length and width. In this case, the width is 3 feet, and the length is twice this amount, so it is 6 feet.

$$A = l \times w$$

$$A = 6 \text{ ft} \times 3 \text{ ft}$$

$$A = 18 \text{ ft}^2$$

Therefore, the area of the tabletop is 18 square feet.

EXAMPLE

The volume of a cube is 64 cubic inches. What is the perimeter of one face of the cube?

16 inches

The volume, V, of a cube is calculated using the formula $V = l \times w \times h$, where l, w, and h represent the length, width, and height of the cube, respectively. Since the solid is a cube, then the length, width, and height are the same value. Test a few values to determine what the side length is: $2 \times 2 \times 2 = 8$, $3 \times 3 \times 3 = 27$, and $4 \times 4 \times 4 = 64$. This means that each edge of the cube is 4 inches. The perimeter of one face of the cube is the sum of 4 edges.

$$4 + 4 + 4 + 4 = 16$$

The perimeter of one face of the cube is 16 inches.

Volume and Cubic Units

All three-dimensional figures occupy space. This space is defined as **volume**. Volume is also known as capacity. Spheres, prisms, pyramids, cylinders, cones, and cubes are common three-dimensional figures that have volume. The volume of a three-dimensional solid is measured in cubic units. For example, a cube has a length, width, and height. A cube that is 1 unit tall, 1 unit wide, and 1 unit deep is called a **unit cube**. The number of unit cubes that fills a solid determines its volume. The formula $V = l \times w \times h$, where l is length, w is width, and h is height, can be used to calculate the volume of a cube or rectangular prism.

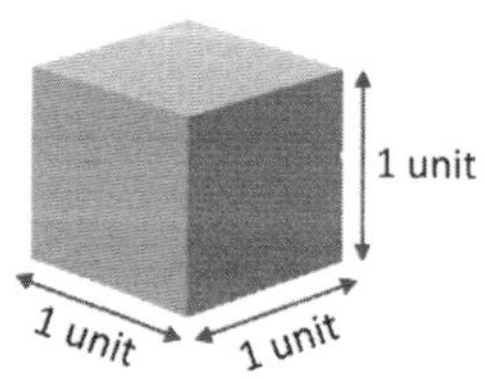

For example, a rectangular prism that is has a height of 4 units, a width of 3 units, and a depth of 6 units has a volume of 4 units × 3 units × 6 units, which is 72 units^3. Remember, this is *not* the volume formula for all three-dimensional solids. Each solid has its own volume formula.

Many solids will have dimensions that give specific units. For example, a cube might have side lengths measured in centimeters, which means the volume would be described as "cubic centimeters," not "cubic units."

Consider the cube below. The side lengths are all 4 centimeters. The volume formula can be applied. $V = l \times w \times h$ becomes $V = 4 \times 4 \times 4$. This simplifies to 64, so the volume of the cube is 64 cm^3. There are 64 total squares in the cube, so the volume is 64 cm^3. Notice how the volume formula takes less time than counting up each individual square.

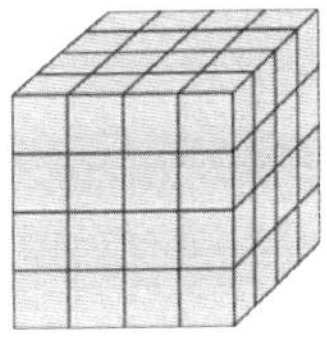

VOLUME OF A RECTANGULAR PRISM

The volume of a rectangular prism can be found in a variety of ways. One option is to simply count every single cube within the prism. This is generally unrealistic because of the amount of time it takes. Another option is to calculate volume based on the number of **layers** within a cube. For example, consider the $5 \times 5 \times 5$ cube below. Notice how there are 5 horizontal layers, and each layer contains 25 unit cubes. There are 5 of these layers, so the total volume can be calculated as 5×25, or 5 groups of 25, which is 125. Therefore, the volume of the cube is 125 cubic units.

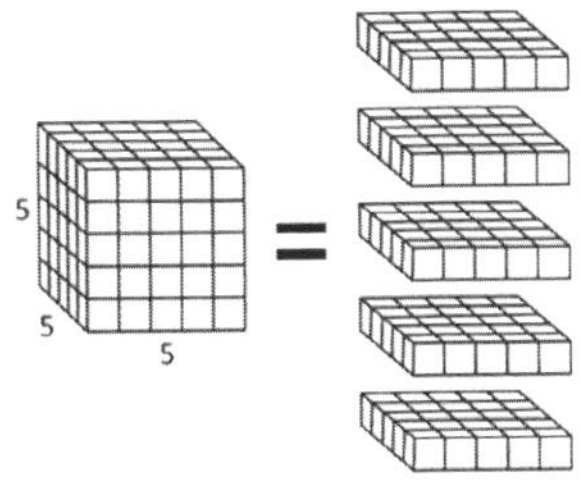

This layering strategy can be applied to cubes and rectangular prisms. For example, the prism below is constructed from 5 horizontal layers. Each layer contains 4 columns and 8 rows. This means that each layer contains 4×8, or 32 unit cubes. Each layer contains 32 unit cubes, and there are 5 layers. Therefore, the total number of unit cubes can be calculated as $5 \times 32 = 160$, or 160 cubic units.

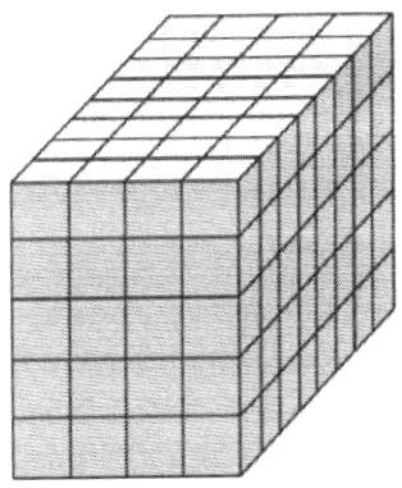

Geometry

Coordinate Planes

The **coordinate plane** is a two-dimensional plane formed from the intersection of a vertical and horizontal line. The horizontal line is referred to as the ***x*-axis**, and the vertical line is referred to as the ***y*-axis**. The x-axis and y-axis are perpendicular to each other. The x-axis and y-axis extend out from the **origin**, which is located at the point (0,0). The coordinate plane is sometimes referred to as a **coordinate plane**, and can be used to describe points, or **ordered pairs**. Ordered pairs consist of an x-coordinate and a y-coordinate. The x-coordinate indicates horizontal movement from the origin, to the right or left. The y-coordinate indicates vertical movement from the origin, up or down. In other words, the x- and y-coordinates reflect how far over and how far up an ordered pair is on the coordinate plane. For example, the point (3,2) has an x-coordinate of 3 and a y-coordinate of 2. The point (3,2) is plotted by moving 3 units to the right and 2 units up from the origin (0,0).

Graphing Ordered Pairs

All ordered pairs take the form (x, y), where x describes the horizontal movement, and y describes the vertical movement. For example, consider the graph below. Start at the origin (0,0). The point (3,5) indicates a movement of 3 units horizontally to the right, and 5 units vertically up. The point (3,5) can be plotted on the coordinate plane.

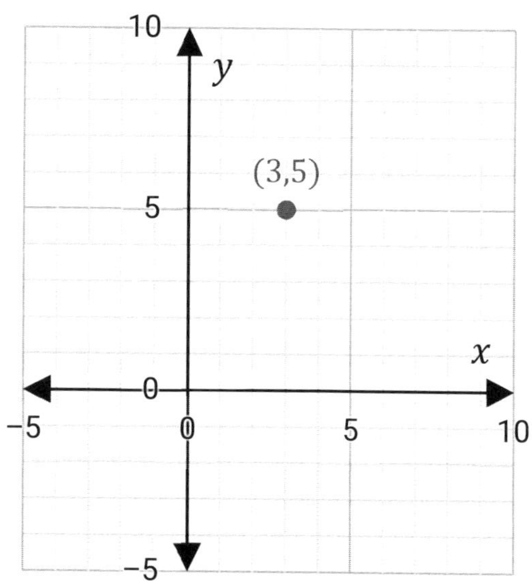

It is important not to swap the x and y locations within an ordered pair. For example, the location of (3,5) is not the same as the location of (5,3).

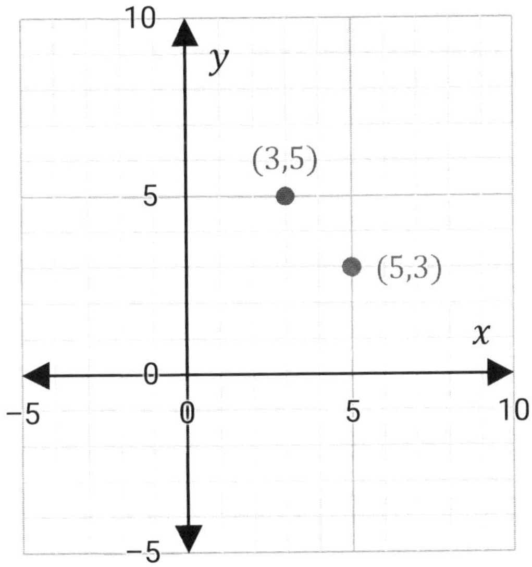

Review Video: Cartesian Coordinate Plane and Graphing
Visit mometrix.com/academy and enter code: 115173

Graphing Ordered Pairs Based on Math and Real-World Problems

Ordered pairs can be generated from real-world problems or problems involving input-output tables. Any problem that includes an independent variable (x-variable) and a dependent variable (y-variable) can be graphed on a coordinate plane.

For example, the input-output table below shows the relationship between glasses of juice and total cost. Each glass of juice costs $3. The cost depends on the number of glasses; therefore, the cost is the dependent variable. This means that the number of glasses will be the x-variable, and the total cost will be the y-variable.

Cups of Juice (x)	0	1	2	3	4
Total Cost (y)	0	3	6	9	12

Each pair of x- and y-values represents an ordered pair that can be plotted on a coordinate plane. Remember, ordered pairs follow the form (x, y). The ordered pairs for this scenario include (0,0), (1,3), (2,6), (3,9), and (4,12).

Classifying Two-Dimensional Figures

Two-dimensional shapes can be classified and sorted based on properties such as number of angles, edges, and vertices. **Polygons** are two-dimensional figures that are formed by straight lines on a flat surface. One way to sort polygons is based on the number of sides they have.

Graphic organizers can be helpful for sorting polygons into categories. Polygons can be split into three categories. One category contains three-sided polygons called **triangles**, one category contains four-sided polygons called **quadrilaterals**, and one category contains polygons with more than four sides. Notice how the number of sides is always the same as the number of angles and vertices.

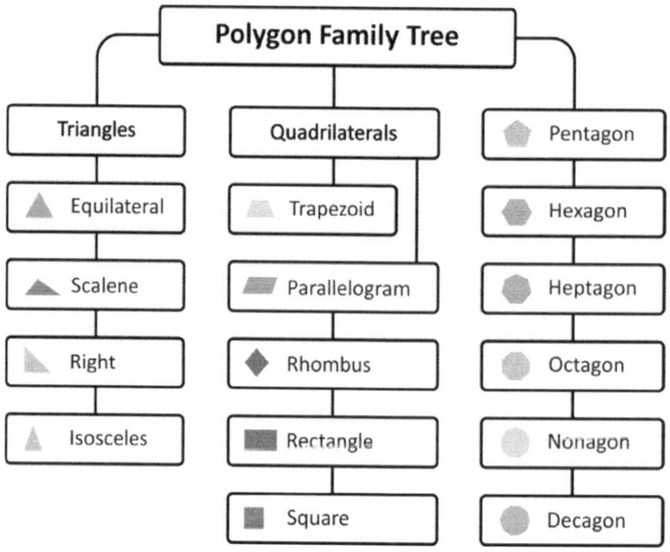

EXAMPLE

Franklin is sorting two-dimensional shapes. He places a rectangle, square, and rhombus into a group, and labels the group "parallelograms." Franklin's friend Henry says that this is incorrect because the group should also contain trapezoids. Is Henry correct?

Henry is not correct. Franklin has labeled the shapes correctly.

Rectangles, squares, and rhombi fall under the umbrella of parallelograms. Parallelograms are defined as four-sided figures with two pairs of opposite sides that are parallel. Trapezoids do not fall into this category because trapezoids only have one set of parallel sides. A trapezoid is shown below.

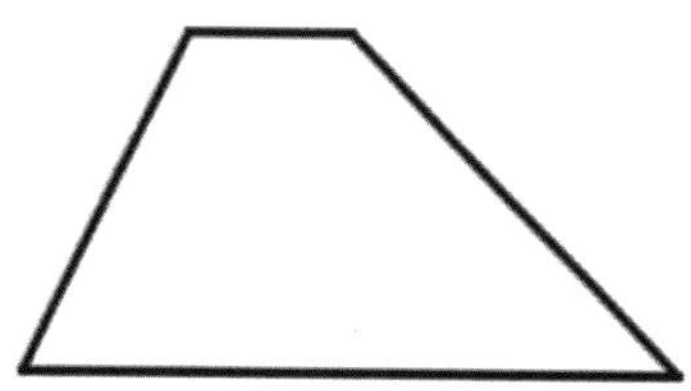

EXAMPLE

Elizabeth states that all squares can be classified as a rhombus, but not all rhombi are classified as squares. Ryan states that all rhombi can be classified as squares, but not all squares can be classified as rhombi. Who is correct?

Elizabeth is correct.

All squares can be classified as a rhombus, but not all rhombi are classified as squares. A square has four congruent sides and four right angles. This qualifies as a rhombus because a rhombus is a four-sided figure with four congruent sides. However, in a rhombus, the angles do not have to be 90 degrees. For example, both figures below can be classified as a rhombus, but only the figure on the left can be classified as a square.

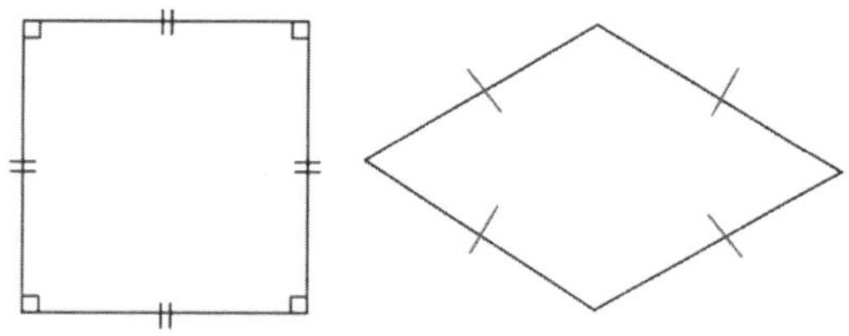

Practice Test #1

1. Simplify the expression using order of operations: $6 + 8 \times (12 \div 4) - 2$

a. 84
b. 40
c. 51
d. 28

2. What is the equivalent decimal number for zero and seven hundred six thousandths?

a. 0.706
b. 0.0706
c. 7.006
d. 7.600

3. Round this decimal to the nearest hundredth: 340.587?

a. 341
b. 340.6
c. 340.59
d. 300

4. The number of customers in a new restaurant is given in the table below.

Week	Customers
1	155
2	180
3	205

What is the rule for the pattern displayed in the table above?

a. $c + 30$
b. $c + 25$
c. $c - 30$
d. $c - 25$

5. Which number represents "fifty-seven thousand and three hundredths"?

a. 57,000.03
b. 57,300.00
c. 5,700.03
d. 57,000.003

6. Part A: Given the figure of the quadrilateral below, which category does the figure belong under?

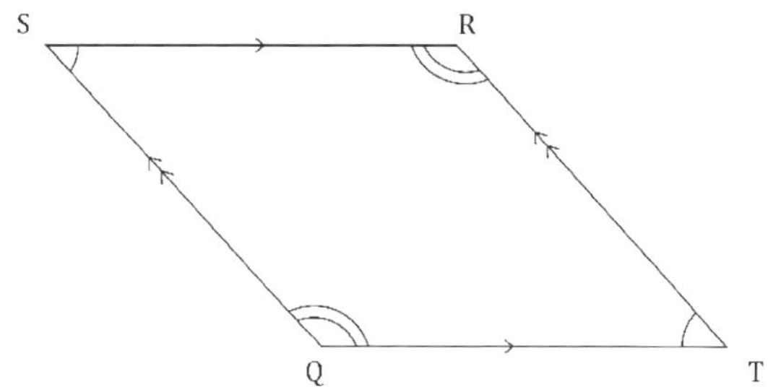

a. Square
b. Parallelogram
c. Rectangle
d. Trapezoid

Part B: What characteristics of the quadrilateral help determine this?

a. four right angles, two sets of congruent sides
b. two sets of parallel sides, no right angles
c. one set of parallel sides
d. four right angles, four congruent sides

7. Round to the nearest tenth in 539.464?

a. 540
b. 539
c. 539.5
d. 539.46

8. The rectangular prism below has a volume of 144 cubic cm. The length and width are given below. What is the height of the rectangular prism?

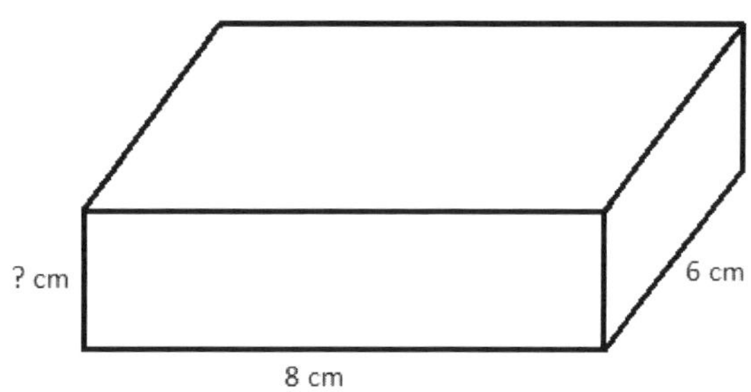

a. 18 cm
b. 3 cm
c. 96 cm
d. 48 cm

9. Find the sum of the decimals below.

$$\begin{array}{r} 6.80 \\ 11.30 \\ +\ \ 0.06 \\ \hline \end{array}$$

a. 17.16
b. 17.70
c. 18.16
d. 18.70

10. The recipe Mary is using to bake cupcakes requires 1 cup of milk and makes 8 cupcakes. If she needs to make 32 cupcakes for the party, how much milk is needed?

a. 1 pint
b. 1 gallon
c. 3 cups
d. 1 quart

11. Solve the equation: $\frac{2}{5}+\frac{3}{4}-\frac{1}{2}=$ ______.

a. $\frac{6}{11}$
b. $\frac{4}{7}$
c. $\frac{31}{20}$
d. $\frac{13}{20}$

12. What is another way to express $14 \div 16$?

a. $\frac{16}{14}$
b. $14 \times \frac{1}{6}$
c. $\frac{14}{16}$
d. $\frac{1}{4} \times 16$

13. Donnie has a baseball card that is $4\frac{1}{5}$ inches tall and $2\frac{3}{5}$ inches wide. What is the area of the card?

a. $10\frac{23}{25}$ in^2
b. $8\frac{4}{5}$ in^2
c. $16\frac{3}{10}$ in^2
d. $54\frac{3}{5}$ in^2

14. An electronics store sells Evercell (E) brand batteries in packages of 4 and Durapower (*D*) brand batteries in packages of 6. Which expression represents the total number of batteries in the store?

a. $(4+E)\times(6+D)$
b. $(4\times E)+(6\times D)$
c. $(4+E)+(6+D)$
d. $(4\times E)\div(6\times D)$

15. At the park there is a walking trail that goes around the perimeter. One lap around the park is 0.28 miles. Samantha walks 11 laps. How far has she walked?

a. 0.308
b. 30.8
c. 3.08
d. 308

16. Solve the equation below.

$$(\mathbf{0.22} + \mathbf{1.48}) \times \mathbf{0.5} =$$

a. 0.96
b. 0.83
c. 0.85
d. 0.63

17. If a chef can make 25 pastries in a day, how many can he make in a week?

a. 32
b. 74
c. 126
d. 175

18. A fish tank is a rectangular prism with a length of 7 inches and a width of 5 inches and can hold a volume of 210 cubic inches of water. What is the height of the tank?

a. 6 inches
b. 5 inches
c. 17.5 inches
d. 10 inches

19. The all-time rushing leader in professional football ran for 18,335 yards in his career. What is the best whole number approximation of the number of miles he ran?

a. 1,500 miles
b. 10 miles
c. 31,680,000 miles
d. 216,000 miles

20. A large pitcher contains $\frac{1}{3}$ gallon of apple juice. If the same amount of juice is poured into 5 glasses, how many gallons of juice will each glass contain?

a. $\frac{1}{15}$ gallons
b. 15 gallons
c. $\frac{1}{3}$ gallons
d. $\frac{1}{5}$ gallons

21. Cindy earned \$100 one week at the ice cream stand. She put $\frac{1}{4}$ of the money in her savings account and kept the rest as cash. After this, she received a cash bonus of \$20 from the owner of the ice cream stand and didn't put any of it in the savings account. Which expression represents the amount of cash Cindy currently has?

a. $C = \frac{3}{4}(100) + 20$
b. $C = \frac{1}{4}(100) + 20$
c. $C = \frac{1}{4}(100) - 20$
d. $C = \frac{3}{4}(120)$

22. Mr. Thompson fills his 25.2 gallon gasoline tank with gas that costs \$2.98 a gallon. Which is the best approximation of the cost of the gasoline?

a. \$50
b. \$60
c. \$75
d. \$90

23. Part A: Using the order of operations solve the problem below.

$$\mathbf{8 \times (5 - 2) + (4 + 5)}$$

a. 47
b. 96
c. 52
d. 33

Part B: What is the first step when following order of operations?

a. Exponents
b. Subtraction
c. Parenthesis/Grouping symbols
d. Multiplication

24. Robin earned \$2,520 from babysitting this month. If she earned \$28 per hour, how many hours did she work this month?

a. 28 hours
b. 84 hours
c. 90 hours
d. 100 hours

25. Jamie is paid \$22 per hour and received a one-time tip of \$50. The variable x represents the number of hours that Jamie worked. The variable y represents the one-time tip of \$50. Which table represents this scenario?

a.

x	y
1	70
2	80
3	90

b.

x	y
1	72
2	94
3	116

c.

x	y
1	72
2	100
3	133

d.

x	y
1	22
2	44
3	66

26. It takes Jack 14.67 minutes to get to school in the morning. It only takes Clayton 10.24 minutes to get to school. How much less time does it take Jack to get to school?

a. 24.91
b. 4.03
c. 1.39
d. 4.43

27. A ship is located on the map at coordinates (4, 9). If the radar indicates the lighthouse is 5 units east and 4 units south of the ship, what is the location of the lighthouse?

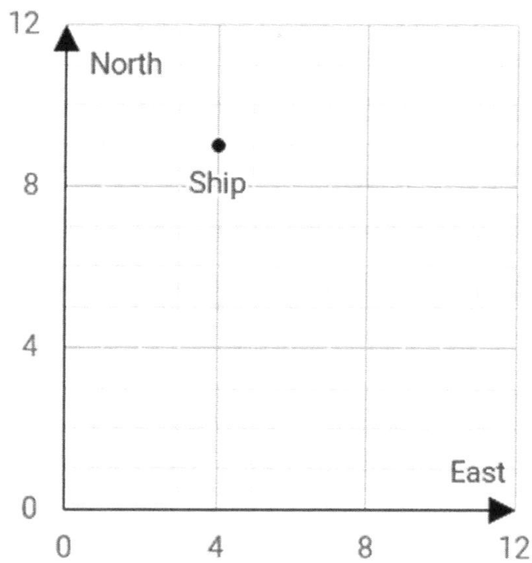

a. (9, 5)
b. (9, 4)
c. (8, 3)
d. (9, 13)

28. Marco's family has 4 dogs. The weight of each dog is listed below. Which two of the following comparisons of dog weight are NOT correct? Select all that apply.

Dog Name	Dog Weight (in pounds)
Franklin	60.34
Willow	55.8
Georgia	60.038
Baxter	56.08

a. Franklin > Georgia
b. Willow > Baxter
c. Baxter < Georgia
d. Georgia < Willow

29. A zoo has three different lion enclosures. The first one is $\frac{5}{8}$ of an acre. The second one is $\frac{5}{6}$ of an acre. If the third one is $\frac{7}{12}$, what is the total number of acres in all three enclosures?

a. $2\frac{1}{24}$
b. $\frac{17}{26}$
c. $\frac{1}{24}$
d. $\frac{49}{72}$

30. On the graph below plot the points A(6,9) and B(3,8).

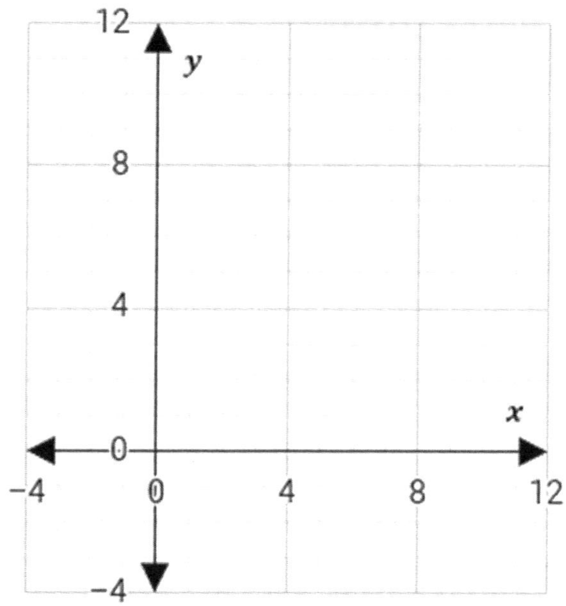

31. What is the value of $6 \div \frac{1}{4}$?

a. 22
b. $\frac{4}{6}$
c. 24
d. $\frac{6}{4}$

32. Cooper built a tower out of unit cubes. Which choice shows a correct way to calculate the volume of the tower?

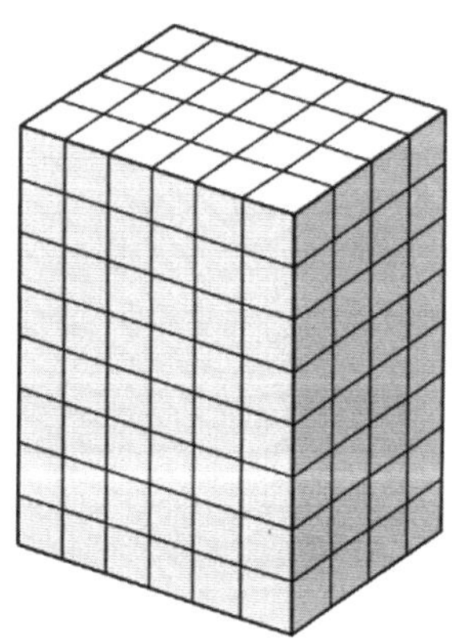

a. $(6 \times 8) + 4 = 52$ cubic units
b. $(6 + 4) \times 8 = 80$ cubic units
c. $(6 \times 4) \times 8 = 192$ cubic units
d. $(6 \times 4) + 8 = 32$ cubic units

33. Anna is a jewelry designer. She can assemble 12 earrings per hour. The equation $y = 12x$ can be used to represent this relationship. Which table represents the rule $y = 12x$?

a.

x	y
1	12
2	13
3	14
4	15

b.

x	y
1	12
2	24
3	30
4	48

c.

x	y
1	12
2	24
3	36
4	48

d.

x	y
0	12
2	24
4	36
6	48

34. Which point lies within the enclosed region below?

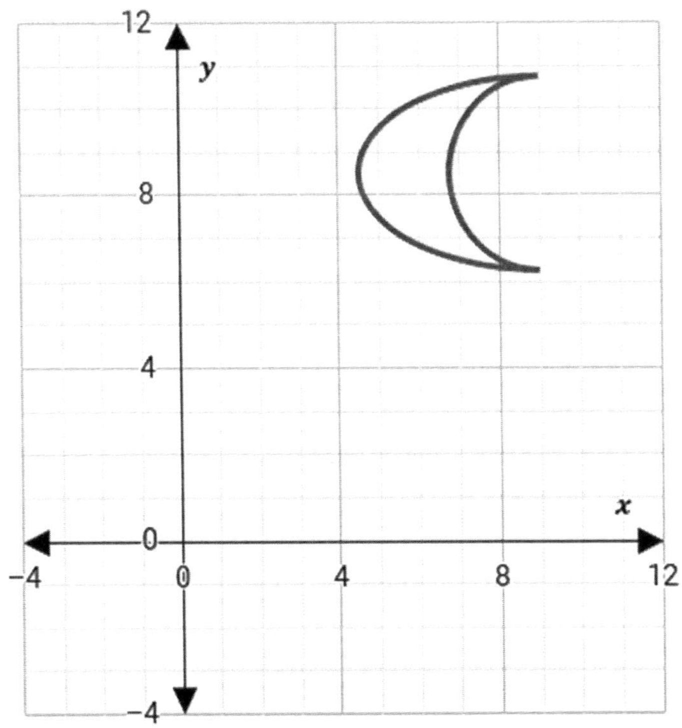

a. (5, 6)
b. (8, 6)
c. (7, 10)
d. (9, 9)

35. The Venn diagram below is set up to sort the polygons A, B, C, and D. Write the letter of each shape where that shape should be placed in the diagram.

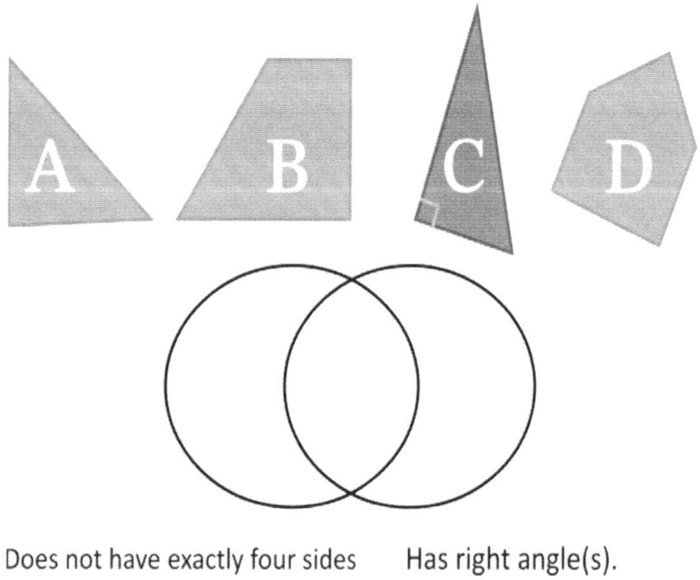

36. Peter earns \$4,025 each year mowing grass. About how much money will Peter earn after 4 years?

a. \$16,080
b. \$16,500
c. \$16,100
d. \$16,400

37. Daniel is simplifying the expression $3(60 + 4) - 11$. Which choice describes the role of the parentheses within the expression?

a. Add 60 and 4 before multiplying by 3.
b. Subtract 11 before adding 60 and 4.
c. Multiply 3 by 11 before adding 60 and 4.
d. Add 4 after multiplying 3 by 60.

38. Sarah was measuring and recording the amount of pie each person took to eat on the dot plot below. Based of the data in the dot plot, how many pies did Sarah's guests eat in total?

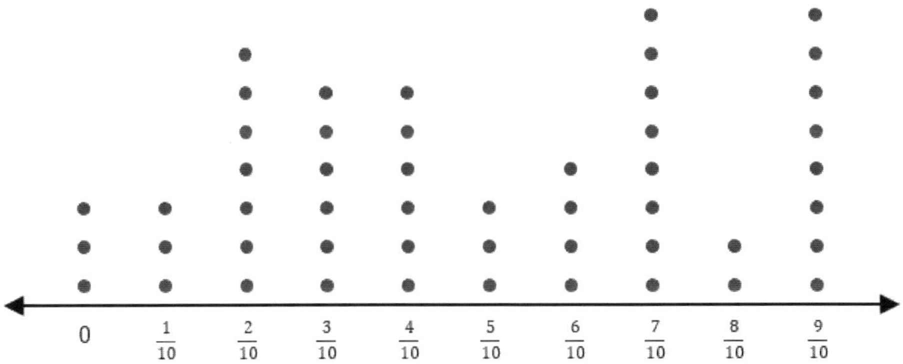

a. $24\frac{1}{5}$
b. $2\frac{31}{45}$
c. $26\frac{8}{9}$
d. $24\frac{1}{2}$

39. Julie shopped for first-aid cream. One large tube held 1.5 fluid ounces and the smallest tube held 0.33 fluid ounces. What is the difference in the number of fluid ounces of cream in the two tubes?

a. 1.8
b. 1.27
c. 1.23
d. 1.17

40. Fill in the point that can be graphed using the following procedures.

1. Start at the origin.
2. Move 6 units to the right.
3. From this location, move 2 units up.

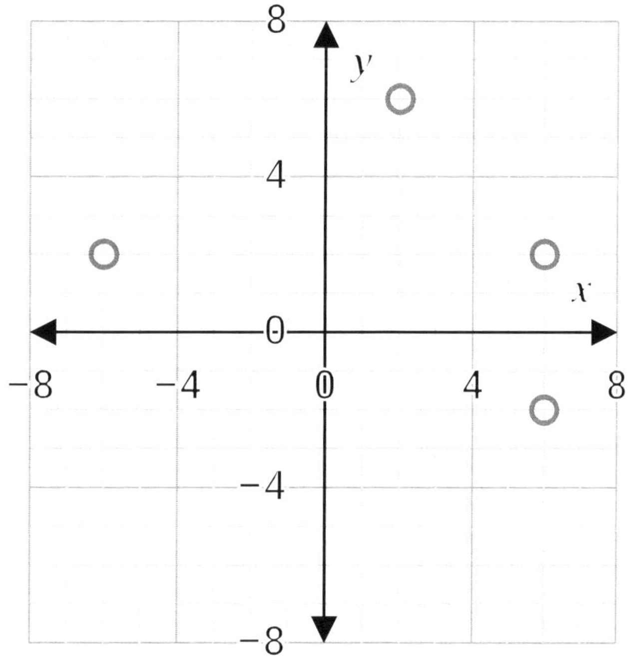

Answers and Explanations for Test #1

1. D: PEMDAS should be used when simplifying expressions. The expression inside the parenthesis will be done first. Then multiplication and division should be performed from left to right. Then addition and subtraction should be performed from left to right.

$$6 + 8 \times (12 \div 4) - 2$$
$$6 + 8 \times 3 - 2$$
$$6 + 24 - 2$$
$$30 - 2$$
$$28$$

2. A: Write 0. The word "and" represents the decimal point. Then write 706, and the last digit should match the correct place value. The 6 is in the thousandths place value, so it is correct.

3. C: The hundredths place is the second digit to the right of a decimal point. In order to round, look at the number to the right of the hundredths place. That digit is a 7. If the number to the right is 5 or greater, round up. If the number to the right is less than 5, round down. Since the number to the right is greater than 5, the rounded answer will be 340.59.

4. B: The pattern in the table is that the number of customers is increasing by 25 each week. Therefore, the number of customers each week is the previous week's value (c) plus 25. For example, $155 + 25 = 180$ customers for week 2, and $180 + 25 = 205$ customers for week 3.

Week	Customers
1	155
2	180
3	205

+25

+25

5. A: Fifty-seven thousand is expressed as the 5 in the ten thousands place and the 7 in the thousands place. The word "and" represents the decimal point. The 3 belongs in the second place to the right of the decimal since it said three hundredths.

6. Part A: B: Squares and rectangles both have four right angles. This quadrilateral does not have right angles. However, it has two sets of parallel sides. Trapezoids have one pair of parallel sides. Thus, this figure is a parallelogram.

Part B: B: Parallelograms have two sets of parallel sides. While a rectangle and a square can also be a parallelogram, these two quadrilaterals also have four right angles. A trapezoid has only one set of parallel sides.

7. C: The tenths place is the first digit to the right of a decimal point. In order to round, look at the number to the right of the tenths place. That digit is a 6. If the number to the right is 5 or greater, round up. If the number to the right is less than 5, round down. Since the number to the right is greater than 5, the rounded answer will be 539.5.

8. B: The area of a rectangular prism is $A = L \times W \times H$. The problem gives *L, W,* and *A*. To get *H* just divide *A* by *L* and *W*. $144 \div 8 = 18 \div 6 = 3$. So *H*=3.

9. C: This is a simple addition problem. Line up the decimals so that they are all in the same place in the equation, and see that there is a 6 by itself in the hundredth's column. Then add the tenths column: $8 + 3 = 11$. Write down the 1 and carry the 1. Add the ones column: $6 + 1$ plus the carried 1. Write down 8. Then write down the 1.

$$\begin{array}{r} 6.8 \\ 11.3 \\ +\ 0.06 \\ \hline \end{array} \qquad \begin{array}{r} +1 \\ 6\ .8 \\ 11\ .3 \\ +\ 0\ .06 \\ \hline 16 \end{array} \qquad \begin{array}{r} +1 \\ 6\ .8 \\ 11\ .3 \\ +\ 0\ .06 \\ \hline 8\ .16 \end{array} \qquad \begin{array}{r} +1 \\ 6\ .8 \\ 11\ .3 \\ +\ 0\ .06 \\ \hline 18\ .16 \end{array}$$

10. D: The recipe is being multiplied by 4 in this problem, therefore $\frac{1}{8} = \frac{4}{32}$ so a total of 4 cups of milk are needed. Since this is not one of the choices, a conversion is needed. 1 pint = 2 cups and 1 quart = 2 pints, therefore 1 quart = 4 cups.

11. D: To solve a problem like this first find a least common denominator. For 2, 4, and 5 that would be 20. Then convert each fraction to twentieths. $\frac{2}{5} = \frac{8}{20}, \frac{3}{4} = \frac{15}{20}, and\ \frac{1}{2} = \frac{10}{20}$. Next perform the operations that were given. $\frac{8}{20} + \frac{15}{20} - \frac{10}{20} = \frac{13}{20}$.

12. C: Another way to express division is through a fraction. The dividend will always be the numerator, and the divisor will always be the denominator. Since 14 is being divided by 16, 14 is the dividend, and 16 is the divisor.

13. A : $A = L \times W$, so multiplying $4\frac{1}{5} \times 2\frac{3}{5} = \frac{21}{5} \times \frac{13}{5} = \frac{273}{25} = 10\frac{23}{25}$. The area of the card is $10\frac{23}{25}$ sq inches.

14. B: The total number of Evercell batteries is $(4 \times E)$ and the total number of Durapower batteries is $(6 \times D)$. The sum of the two is the total number of batteries in the store.

15. C: To find the total distance multiply the number of laps times the distance of one lap. $11 \times 0.28 = 3.08$

16. C: Follow order of operations and apply decimal operation rules.

$$(0.22 + 1.48) \times 0.5 = (1.7) \times 0.5 = 0.85$$

17. D: Knowing that the chef can make 25 pastries in a day and that there are 7 days in a week, the weekly number can be calculated by multiplying 25 by 7.

$$25 \times 7 = 175$$

Therefore, the chef can make 175 pastries in a week

18. A: The rectangular prism volume formula $V = l \times w \times h$ is used here.

$210 = 7 \times 5 \times h$. Dividing both sides by 35 gives the answer $h = 6$ inches.

19. B: Divide the number of yards by 1760, the number of yards in 1 mile.

$\frac{18335}{1760} \approx 10.42$ miles. Rounded to the nearest whole number is 10 miles.

20. A: $\frac{1}{3}$ gallon of apple juice is poured into 5 glasses. This represents a division scenario, $\frac{1}{3}$ is divided into 5 equal groups. Use the strategy of "Keep, Change, Flip" to calculate $\frac{1}{3} \div 5$. Keep the first value the same. Keep $\frac{1}{3}$ as $\frac{1}{3}$. Change the $\div$ symbol to a $\times$ symbol. Flip the second value. 5 becomes $\frac{1}{5}$, and $\frac{1}{3} \div 5$ becomes $\frac{1}{3} \times \frac{1}{5}$. To multiply fractions, multiply the numerators together and the denominators together, resulting in $\frac{1}{15}$. Each glass will contain $\frac{1}{15}$ gallons of juice.

21. A: $C = \frac{3}{4}(100) + 20$. Since $\frac{1}{4}$ of the original \$100 was sent to the savings account, $\frac{3}{4}$ of the money was kept in cash. The bonus was then added afterward.

22. C: Use approximation to solve this problem quickly: $25 \times \$3 = \$75$. The actual cost to fill the tank was $25.2 \times \$2.98 = \$75.10$.

23. Part A: D: The order of operations is parentheses, exponents, multiply, divide, add, subtract. So for this problem it would be: $8 \times (5 - 2) + (4 + 5) = 8 \times 3 + 9 = 24 + 9 = 33$

Part B: C: When following order of operations, the term PEMDAS or GEMDAS can be helpful. Operations inside the parenthesis/grouping symbols, exponents, multiplication and division from left to right, and then addition and subtraction from left to right.

24. C: Robin earned \$2,520 total and earned \$28 per hour. This represents a division scenario. The total number of hours can be calculated by dividing the total amount of money earned by the amount of money earned per hour. $2{,}520 \div 28$ can be solved using the long division algorithm.

```
      90
  28)2520
    -252
      00
     - 0
       0
```

28 is too large to fit into 2. 28 is too large to fit into 25. 28 fits into 252 nine times. Write 9 above the farthest place value to the right within the number 252.

$9 \times 28 = 252$. Subtract and bring down the next digit, which is 0.

28 goes into 0 zero times. Write 0 below 0. $0 \times 28 = 0$. Subtract. There are no remainders.

The quotient of 2,520 and 28 is 90, so Robin worked 90 hours this month.

25. B: Jamie earns \$22 per hour, and a \$50 tip. In order to determine the amount of money Jamie earns, the number of hours should be multiplied by 22 and then added to 50. The only table that matches this pattern is table B.

$$(1 \times 22) + 50 = 72$$

$$(2 \times 22) + 50 = 94$$

$$(3 \times 22) + 50 = 116$$

26. D: When a problem asks for the difference use subtraction. $14.67 - 10.24 = 4.43$.

27. A: Translate the point 5 units to the right and 4 units down to find the location of the lighthouse.

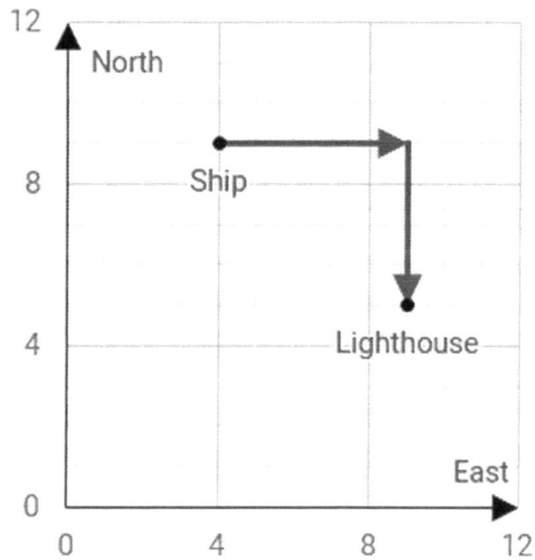

28. B, D: When comparing decimal values, compare each place value one at a time from left to right.

6	0.	3	4		Franklin
6	0.	0	3	4	Georgia
5	6.	0	8		Baxter
5	5.	8			Willow

Franklin and Georgia have the same digits in the tens and ones places. However, Franklin has a larger digit in the tenths place. This means that Franklin is the heaviest dog. Georgia is the second heaviest dog.

Baxter and Willow have the same digit in the tens place, but Baxter has a larger digit in the ones place. This means that Baxter is heavier than Willow. Baxter is the third heaviest dog, and Willow is the fourth heaviest dog.

6	0.	3	4		Franklin
6	0.	0	3	4	Georgia
5	6.	0	8		Baxter
5	5.	8			Willow

$$60.34 > 60.034 > 56.08 > 55.8$$

Franklin > Georgia > Baxter > Willow

Recall, the symbol > means, "greater than," and the symbol < means, "less than." The comparisons Franklin > Georgia and Baxter < Georgia are true. Willow is the least heavy dog and Baxter is the second least heavy dog, so Baxter is heavier than Willow. Willow > Baxter is not true because 55.8 is not greater than 56.08. Georgia is the second heaviest dog and Willow is the least heavy dog. This means that Georgia is heavier than Willow. Georgia < Willow is not true because 60.034 is not less than 55.8.

29. A: To find the total you will also need to first find like denominators. In this case 24 will work. So, $\frac{7}{12} = \frac{14}{24}$, then $\frac{15}{24} + \frac{20}{24} + \frac{14}{24} = \frac{49}{24} = 2\frac{1}{24}$

30.

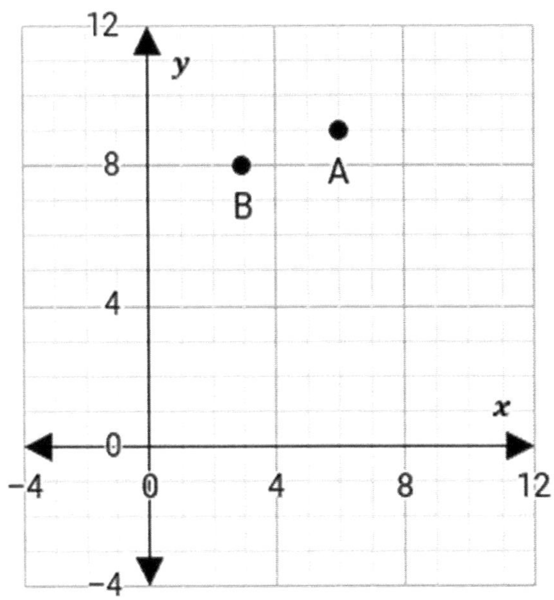

31. C: $6 \div \frac{1}{4}$ can be visualized as 6 wholes being divided into groups of $\frac{1}{4}$. In other words, each whole will be divided into 4 pieces. This results in 24 equal shares of $\frac{1}{4}$. So, $6 \div \frac{1}{4} = 24$.

Another way to solve $6 \div \frac{1}{4}$ is to use the strategy of "Keep, Change, Flip." Keep the first value the same. Keep the 6 as a 6. Change the $\div$ symbol to a $\times$ symbol. Flip the second value so that $\frac{1}{4}$ becomes $\frac{4}{1}$. This results in $\frac{6}{1} \times \frac{4}{1}$. To multiply fractions, multiply the numerators together and the denominators together, resulting in $\frac{24}{1}$, or 24.

32. C: One way to calculate the total number of unit cubes in Cooper's tower is to determine the number of cubes in one layer, and then multiply this value by the number of layers. In this case, there are 6×4 unit cubes in one layer. There are 8 layers in the tower, so $(6 \times 4) \times 8$ will result in the total number of unit cubes.

The total number of unit cubes in the tower represents the volume of the tower. In this case, $(6 \times 4) \times 8$ simplifies to 192, so the volume of the tower is 192 cubic units.

33. C: Anna can assemble 12 earrings in 1 hour.

$$y = 12(1) = 12$$

This means that in 2 hours Anna can assemble 24 earrings, and in 3 hours Anna can assemble 36 earrings.

$$y = 12(2) = 24$$
$$y = 12(3) = 36$$

The pattern continues. The number of earrings assembled is determined by multiplying the number of hours worked by 12. The equation $y = 12x$ represents this rule, and choice C is the only table correctly displaying this relationship.

34. C: The points are marked on the figure below. The only ordered pair that lies inside the enclosed region is (7,10).

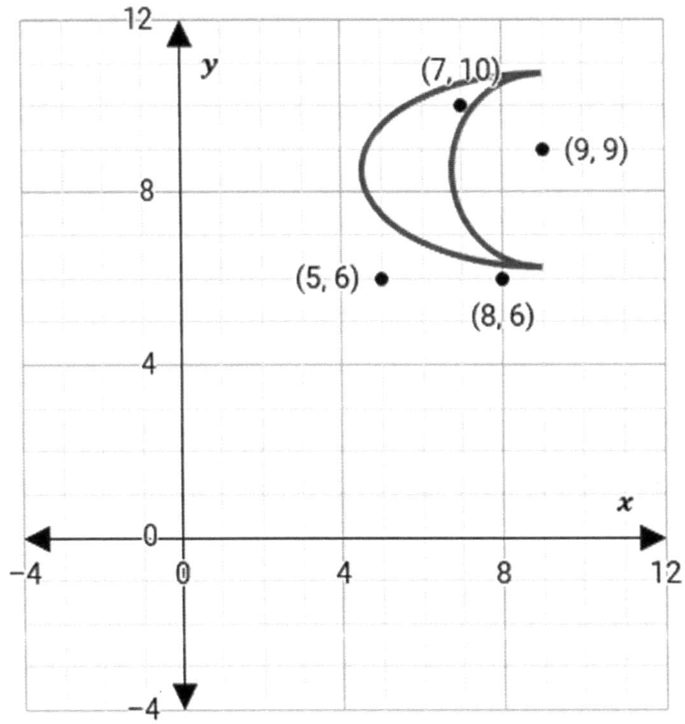

35. Shapes placed in the overlapping middle section of the Venn diagram need to apply to both rules: does not have four sides, and has right angle(s). The only shapes that do not have four sides and have right angle(s), are shapes C and D. Shape A cannot be placed in the middle section because it does not contain right angles, but it does go in the left section because it does not have exactly four sides. Shape B cannot be placed in the middle section because it has four sides, but can be placed in the right section because it does have two right angles.

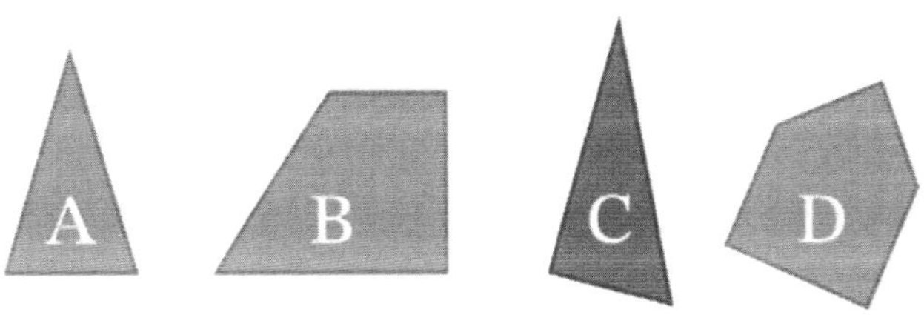

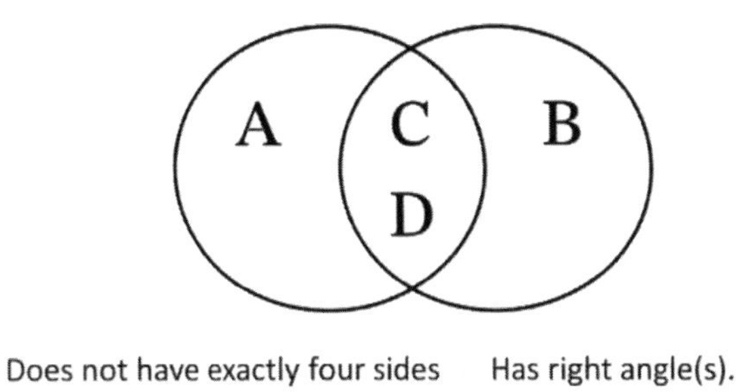

36. C: Peter earns \$4,025 per year. Multiply this number by 4 using the standard algorithm to find the amount he will have earned after 4 years.

$$\begin{array}{r} {}^{1}\;{}^{2} \\ 4\;0\;2\;5 \\ \times\quad\quad\;\; 4 \\ \hline 1\;6\;1\;0\;0 \end{array}$$

37. A: Parentheses and brackets act as grouping symbols within expressions. These grouping symbols are used to represent which section of an expression to simplify first. In this case, the parentheses around $60 + 4$ indicates that 60 needs to be added to 4 before multiplying the sum by 3, and then subtracting 11.

38. A: One person is represented by a dot on the dot plot. There was a total of 50 guests. To figure out how pies Sarah's guest ate, the following expression can be used.

$$3(0) + 3\left(\frac{1}{10}\right) + 7\left(\frac{2}{10}\right) + 6\left(\frac{3}{10}\right) + 6\left(\frac{4}{10}\right) + 3\left(\frac{5}{10}\right) + 4\left(\frac{6}{10}\right) + 8\left(\frac{7}{10}\right) + 2\left(\frac{8}{10}\right) + 8\left(\frac{9}{10}\right)$$

This simplifies to the following:

$$0 + \frac{3}{10} + \frac{14}{10} + \frac{18}{10} + \frac{24}{10} + \frac{15}{10} + \frac{24}{10} + \frac{56}{10} + \frac{16}{10} + \frac{72}{10}$$

To add fractions with like denominators, keep the denominators the same and add all the numerators: $\frac{242}{10}$. Then simplify the fraction back into a mixed number: $24\frac{2}{10}$ or $24\frac{1}{5}$.

39. D: To find the difference, subtract. It is important to align decimal places. Note, when subtracting here, the digit in the hundredths place in 0.33 has no digit aligned above it. We must add a zero to 1.5 so that we can align the hundredths places correctly. Now we can subtract 33 hundredths from the 50 hundredths to get 17 hundredths. So, we get 1.17 as our correct answer.

40. Because we are starting at the origin and moving 6 places to the right and 2 places up, this represents the ordered pair (6,2). The first number listed in an ordered pair represents the x-value, or the horizontal movement from the origin. The second number listed in an ordered pair represents the y-value, or the vertical movement from the origin. The ordered pair (6,2) indicates a horizontal movement of 6 and a vertical movement of 2. This matches the given procedures. $(-6,2)$

and $(6, -2)$ are incorrect due to the negative values. Negative values are not graphed in the first quadrant. (2,6)is incorrect because the x- and y-values are switched.

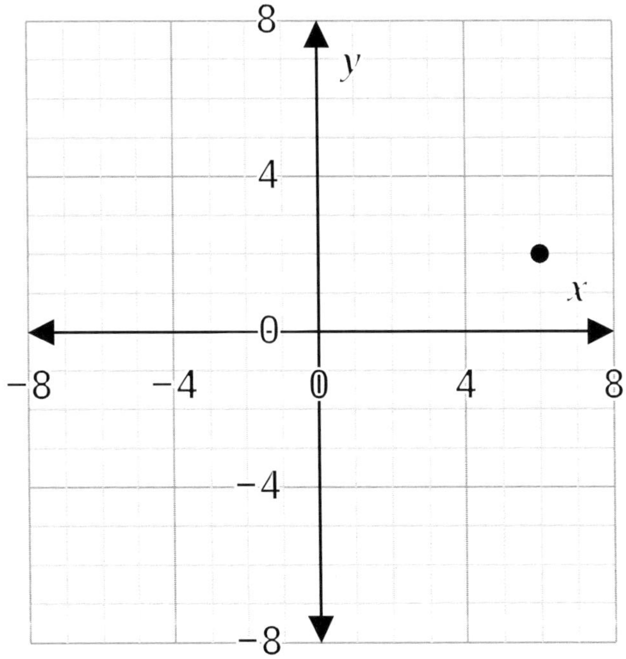

Practice Test #2

1. Find the difference:

$$0.580 - 0.391$$

a. 0.189
b. 0.211
c. 0.299
d. 0.199

2. Part A: The amount Larry pays for each of his audio books is shown on the table below:

Books, b	1	2	3	4	5
Cost, c	9	18	27	36	45

Which equation below represents this relationship?

a. $b = 9c$
b. $c = 9b$
c. $b = c + 9$
d. $c = b + 9$

Part B: What is the cost if Larry purchased 27 books?

a. 36
b. 3
c. 216
d. 243

3. Coach Ryan is purchasing basketball jerseys for his players. He purchases 3 large jerseys, 6 medium jerseys, and 2 small jerseys. What is the total cost of the jerseys?

Jersey Size	Jersey Price
Small	$18.99
Medium	$22.50
Large	$23.95

a. $244.83
b. $249.83
c. $254.83
d. $344.83

4. Mrs. May has 7 chocolate bars. She gives each student in her class $\frac{1}{3}$ of a chocolate bar. How many students are in Mrs. May's class?

a. 21 students
b. $\frac{7}{3}$ students
c. 28 students
d. 24 students

5. An art supply company is shipping out boxes loaded with small tubes of paint. Each box contains 145 tubes of paint. If the art supply company ships 25 boxes, how many tubes of paint are shipped?

a. 3,500 tubes
b. 3,602 tubes
c. 3,622 tubes
d. 3,625 tubes

6. Dennis weighs 56 pounds. His little brother Donny weighs 23 pounds less than him. What is Donny's weight in ounces?

a. 896
b. 528
c. 368
d. 33

7. Find the sum of the following: $6.8 + 11.3 + 0.06$

a. 17.16
b. 17.70
c. 18.16
d. 18.70

8. Simplify the expression using order of operations.

$$64 - 12 \times 3 + 8 - (16 - 4) + 2$$

a. 26
b. 154
c. 22
d. 146

9. Round the decimal below to the nearest hundredth.

$$3.116 \approx$$

a. 3.11
b. 3.12
c. 3.1
d. 3.2

10. Which of the following quadrilaterals is a trapezoid?

a.

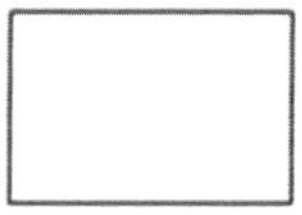

b.

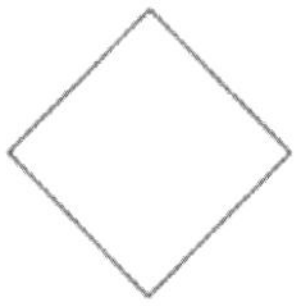

c.

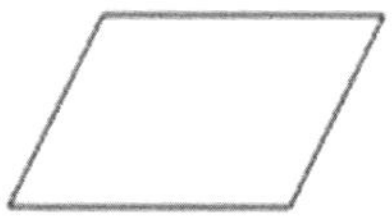

d.

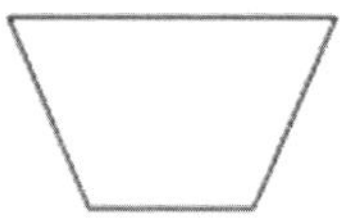

11. A gallon of cooking oil is used to make popcorn for 256 people. How much cooking oil is needed to make popcorn for 96 people? Select all that apply.

a. 2 quarts
b. 3 pints
c. 1 quart
d. 1 cup
e. 48 ounces

12. A new fitness center charges Randy by the number of minutes he works out each day plus an additional fee. This is represented by the table below:

Minutes m	5	10	15	20	25
Cost c	9	14	19	24	29

Which equation represents the relationship shown in the table

a. $c = m + 4$
b. $c = m + 5$
c. $m = c + 4$
d. $m = c + 5$

13. Find the sum of $3.5 + 10.3 + 0.63$.

a. 11.28
b. 13.58
c. 14.43
d. 20.10

14. Anna was given $\frac{1}{2}$ of a cake to take to her family. Bonnie was given $\frac{1}{4}$ of the same cake to take to her family. How much cake was Carol left with?

a. $\frac{3}{4}$
b. $\frac{1}{4}$
c. $\frac{1}{2}$
d. $\frac{1}{3}$

15. Round the decimal to the nearest hundredth: 0.1673

a. 0.16
b. 0.166
c. 0.167
d. 0.17

16. A zoo has three different lion enclosures. The first one is $\frac{5}{8}$ of an acre. The second one is $\frac{5}{6}$ of an acre. How much bigger is the second one than the first one?

a. $\frac{5}{24}$
b. 5
c. $2\frac{1}{2}$
d. $\frac{5}{7}$

17. An employer is dividing a $5,000 bonus evenly between 20 employees. What is the amount each employee receives?

a. $200
b. $500
c. $250
d. $150

18. A large rectangular-prism-shaped tank at the zoo is 8 feet wide and 5 feet high. How long is the tank if it holds a volume of 200 cubic feet of water?

a. 8 feet
b. 6 feet
c. 13 feet
d. 5 feet

19. Mount McKinley, the tallest mountain in North America, is 20,320 feet high. Approximately how many miles tall is the Mount?

a. 6
b. 5
c. 4
d. 3

20. What is the equivalent decimal number for two-hundred eight and four hundred two thousandths?

a. 208.402
b. 2,084.02
c. 20,840.2
d. 208,402

21. A grocery store determines the price of a gallon milk, *P*, in dollars will be determined by multiplying the wholesale price, *W*, in dollars by 1.5 and adding 25 cents. Which expression below represents this relationship?

a. $P = 1.5 + W + 0.25$
b. $P = 0.25W + 1.5$
c. $P = 1.75W$
d. $P = 1.5W + 0.25$

22. Two-dimensional polygons are sorted within the Venn diagram below. Based on the diagram, what could the section on the left be labeled?

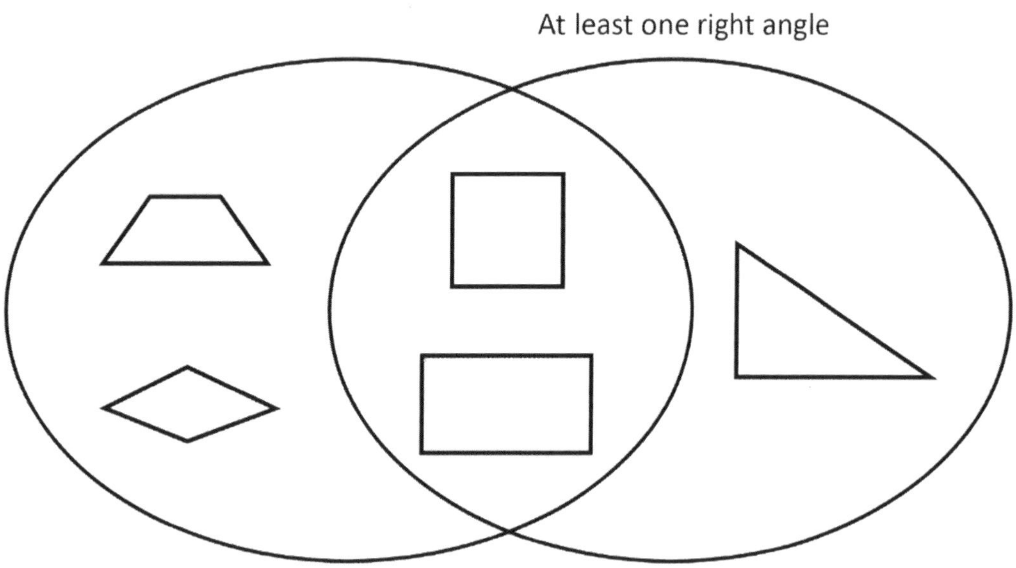

a. At least one right angle
b. Two sets of parallel sides
c. At least one set of parallel sides
d. At least three acute angles

23. Using order of operations simplify the problem below.

$$3 + (9 - 4) \times (4 + 5)$$

a. 1
b. 48
c. 37
d. 72

24. Craig lives in Portland and needs to attend a business meeting in Seattle. The train from Portland to Seattle covers a distance of 145.8 miles. If Craig rides the train from Portland to Seattle, and then back to Portland after the meeting, how many miles has he traveled?

a. 145.8
b. 218.7
c. 291.6
d. 437.6

25. Use the graph to correctly plot the data shown in the input-output table.

x	y
10	6
11	12
12	18
13	24

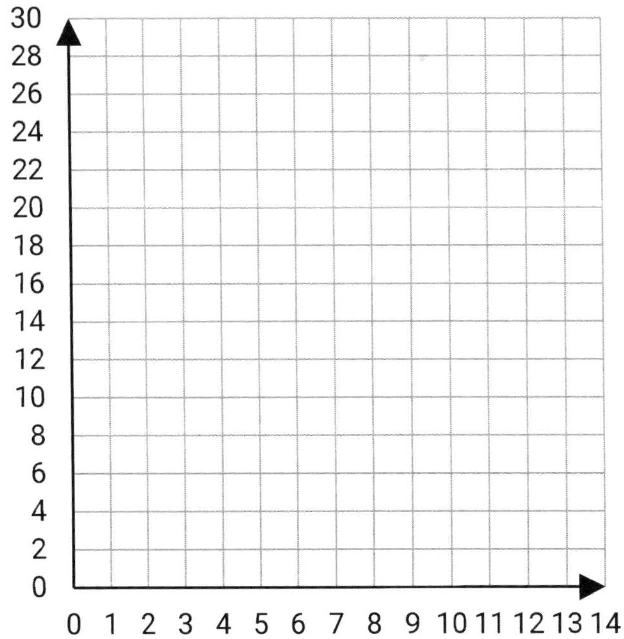

26. Madison writes the numerical expression $[60(20-3)]+1$. Based on the grouping symbols, what is the correct order in which to solve the expression?

a. Subtract 3 from 20, then divide the result by 60. Then add 1.
b. Subtract 3 from 20, then add 1. Then multiply the result by 60.
c. Subtract 3 from 20, then multiply the result by 60. Then add 1.
d. Subtract 3 from 20, then multiply the result by 60.

27. An observation tower is located at point (8, 5) on the map grid below. A fire is observed from a location 4 units west and 2 units north of the tower. What is the location of the fire?

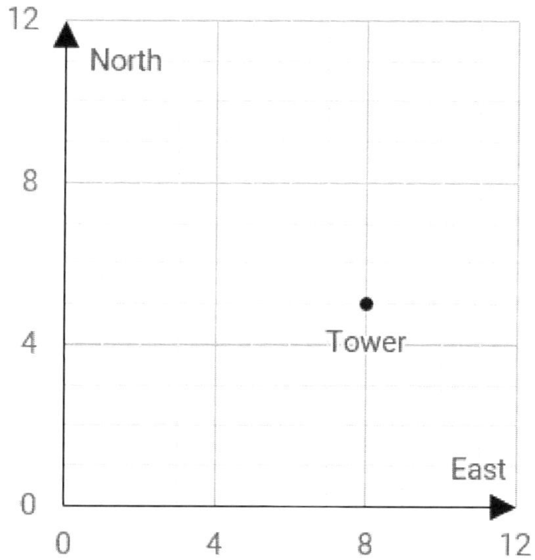

a. (12,7)
b. (4,7)
c. (6,9)
d. (4,5)

28. Maria is moving and needs a box to pack books in. The box needs to be 416 cubic inches. Which of the following boxes is the right size?

a. a box that is 8 $in.\times$ 12 $in.\times$ 5 $in.$
b. a box that is 12 $in.\times$ 4 $in.\times$ 9 $in.$
c. a box that is 13 $in.\times$ 5 $in.\times$ 7 $in.$
d. a box that is 13 $in.\times$ 4 $in.\times$ 8 $in.$

29. Rylie baked cakes for a fundraiser. Baking all of the cakes required 3 cups of brown sugar. Each cake required $\frac{1}{4}$ cup of brown sugar. How many cakes did Rylie bake for the fundraiser?

a. 10 cakes
b. 11 cakes
c. 12 cakes
d. 13 cakes

30. Find the product of the following two factors.

$$0.28 \times 0.17$$

a. 0.2260
b. 0.4760
c. 0.0226
d. 0.0476

31. Chef Xi and Chef Shi are baking pies for a large New Year's Eve celebration. Chef Xi bakes 6 pies every hour for 4 hours. Chef Shi bakes twice as many pies as Chef Xi. When Chef Xi and Chef Shi arrive at the New Year's Eve event with their pies, the host has an additional 7 pies. Which expression represents the total number of pies at the event?

a. $2(6 \times 4)$
b. $2(6 \times 4) + (6 \times 4) + 7$
c. $2(6 \times 4) - 7$
d. $2 \times 6 \times 4 + 7$

32. Which two choices describe the origin of a coordinate plane? Select all that apply.

a. The starting point for graphing any line.
b. The point (0,0).
c. The location on a coordinate plane where the x- and y-axis intersect.
d. The upper right region of the coordinate plane where x- and y-values are both positive.
e. The point where two lines intersect.

33. Frank is selling snacks at a basketball game. A customer purchases 3 bags of popcorn and 2 hotdogs. If the customer pays for the snacks using four 5-dollar bills, how much is the customer owed in change?

Item	Price
Hotdog	\$2.50
Chips	\$1.50
Popcorn bag	\$3.90

a. \$2.30
b. \$3.35
c. \$3.30
d. \$3.70

34. What is the value of $\frac{1}{7} \div 3$?

a. 21
b. $\frac{7}{3}$
c. $\frac{1}{24}$
d. $\frac{1}{21}$

35. Which point lies within the enclosed region below?

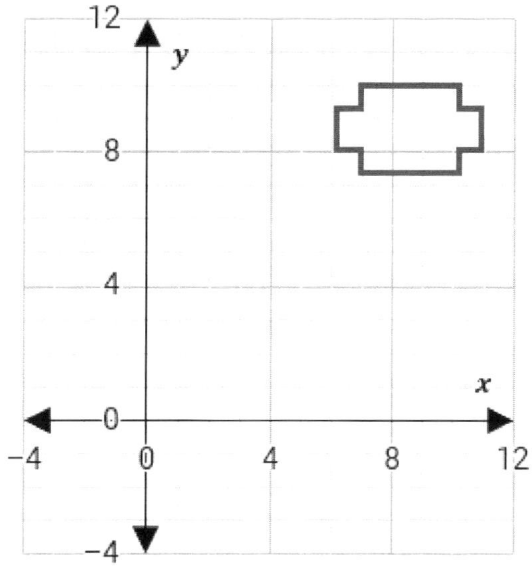

a. (5, 8)
b. (8, 9)
c. (7, 11)
d. (9, 7)

36. A rectangle is $3\frac{2}{5}$ inches wide by $5\frac{7}{10}$ inches long. What is the area in square inches?

a. $18\frac{1}{5}$ in^2
b. $16\frac{4}{5}$ in^2
c. $19\frac{19}{50}$ in^2
d. $17\frac{7}{25}$ in^2

37. Each small cube within the rectangular prism below has a volume of 1 cubic unit. The rectangular prism has a volume of ___ cubic units.

a. 165
b. 160
c. 184
d. 170

38. Which of the following statements correctly compares the decimal numbers 0.24, 0.237, and 0.2366?

a. $0.2366 < 0.24 < 0.237$
b. $0.24 < 0.237 < 0.2366$
c. $0.237 < 0.2366 < 0.24$
d. $0.2366 < 0.237 < 0.24$

39. Which of the following represents five hundred twelve thousandths?

a. 0.512
b. 0.0512
c. 5120.
d. 0.00512

40. What is the product of the following: $3 \times \frac{6}{7}$

a. $2\frac{4}{7}$
b. $\frac{2}{7}$
c. $1\frac{4}{7}$
d. $\frac{3}{7}$

Answers and Explanations for Test #2

1. A: This is a simple subtraction problem with decimals. Line up the decimals and subtract 1 from 0. Since this can't be done, borrow 10 from the 8. Cross out the 8 and make it 7. Now subtract 1 from 10 to get 9. Subtract 9 from 7. Since this can't be done, borrow 10 from the 5. Cross out the 5 and make it 4. Now Subtract 9 from 17 to get 8. Then subtract 3 from 4 and get 1. Place the decimal point before the 1.

2. Part A: B: This table represents a multiplicative relationship. When looking at tables, it is important to analyze what is happening between the two different categories. Each book costs 9 dollars, so the amount of audio books (b) will be multiplied by 9 to find the total cost (c).

Part B: D: Using the equation $c = 9b$, substitute 27 for b, the amount of books purchased. $c = 9(27) = 243$.

3. A: Coach Ryan purchased 3 large jerseys that cost \$23.95 each. The cost of the large jerseys can be determined by multiplying 3×23.95.

$$\begin{array}{r} {}^{1\,2}\ \ {}^{1}\ \ \\ 23.95 \\ \times \quad 3 \\ \hline 71.85 \end{array}$$

Coach Ryan purchased 6 medium jerseys that cost \$22.50 each. The cost of the of the medium jerseys can be determined by multiplying 6×22.50.

$$\begin{array}{r} {}^{1\,3}\ \ \ \ \ \ \\ 22.50 \\ \times \quad 6 \\ \hline 135.00 \end{array}$$

Coach Ryan purchased 2 small jerseys that cost \$18.99 each. The cost of the medium jerseys can be determined by multiplying 2×18.99.

$$\begin{array}{r} {}^{1\,1}\ \ \ \ \ \ \\ 18.99 \\ \times \quad 2 \\ \hline 37.98 \end{array}$$

Coach Ryan's total payment will be the sum of the price of all small, medium, and large jerseys purchased.

$71.85 + 135.00 + 37.98 = 244.83$. Coach Ryan spent \$244.83 on the basketball jerseys.

4. A: Mrs. May is dividing 7 chocolate bars into groups of $\frac{1}{3}$. In other words, Mrs. May is dividing 7 by $\frac{1}{3}$. This can be visualized as 7 wholes that are each divided into 3 equal shares. When 7 bars are sliced into 3 pieces each, the result is 21 small pieces. This means that $7 \div \frac{1}{3} = 21$.
Another way to calculate $7 \div \frac{1}{3}$ is to use the process of "Keep, Change, Flip." Keep 7 as 7. Change $\div$ to $\times$. Flip $\frac{1}{3}$ to $\frac{3}{1}$. So, $7 \div \frac{1}{3}$ becomes $7 \times \frac{3}{1}$. The result is $\frac{21}{1}$, or 21. This means that Mrs. May will have 21 pieces of chocolate. 21 pieces of chocolate indicates that there are 21 students in the class.

5. D: There are 25 boxes, and each box contains 145 tubes of paint. 25 groups of 145 represents a multiplication scenario. The standard algorithm for multiplication can be applied to find the product of 145 and 25.

Multiply the 5 in 25 by each digit in 145.

5 × 5 is 25. Write the 2 above the 4 in 145. Write the 5 on the answer line.

5 × 4 is 20. Add the 2 from above. The result is 22. Write the 2 above the 1 in 145. Write the other 2 on the answer line.

5 × 1 is 5. Add the 2 from above. The result is 7. Write 7 on the answer line.

$$\begin{array}{r} {\scriptstyle 2\,2} \\ 145 \\ \times\ 25 \\ \hline 725 \end{array}$$

Repeat the same process for the digit 2 in 25. Don't forget to include a "place holder zero" in the ones place. This ensures that the place values are lined up correctly.

$$\begin{array}{r} {\scriptstyle 1} \\ 145 \\ \times\ 25 \\ \hline 725 \\ 2900 \end{array}$$

Add both products. In this case, 725 and 2,900. The sum is 3,625. This means that the product of 145 and 24 is 3,625, so 3,625 tubes of paint are shipped.

$$\begin{array}{r} 145 \\ \times\ 25 \\ \hline 725 \\ +\ 2900 \\ \hline 3{,}625 \end{array}$$

6. B: First find Donny's weight in pounds. So, 56-23=33, then it can be converted to ounces by multiplying times 16. $33 \times 16 = 528$.

7. C: This is a simple addition problem. Line up the decimals so that they are all in the same place in the equation, and see that there is a 6 by itself in the hundredth's column. Then add the tenths column: $8 + 3 = 11$. Write down the 1 and carry the 1. Add the ones column: $6 + 1$ plus the carried 1. Write down 8. Then write down the 1.

8. A: PEMDAS should be used when simplifying expressions. The expression inside the parenthesis will be done first. Then multiplication and division should be performed from left to right. Then addition and subtraction should be performed from left to right.

$$64 - 12 \times 3 + 8 - (16 - 4) + 2$$

$$64 - 12 \times 3 + 8 - (12) + 2$$

$$64 - 36 + 8 - (12) + 2$$

$$28 + 8 - (12) + 2$$

$$36 - (12) + 2$$

$$24 + 2$$

$$26$$

9. B: The hundredths place is the second number after the decimal point. When rounding 1-4 rounds down and 5-9 rounds up.

$$3.116 \approx 3.12$$

10. D: A trapezoid is a quadrilateral with only one pair of opposite sides parallel.

The other three figures in the problem are a rectangle, a rhombus, and a parallelogram (in that order).

11. B, E: The proportion given is that 1 gallon of cooking oil will make enough popcorn for 256 people, or 128 ounces serves 256 people. Notice that the amount of oil in ounces needed is exactly one half the number of people being served. This means 48 ounces are needed to serve 96 people. The equivalent amount listed in the choices is 3 pints.

12. A: This table shows an additive relationship. When looking at tables, it is important to analyze what is happening between the two different categories. Randy is charged an additional 4 dollars for plus a dollar for each minute he works out. Therefore, the amount of minutes worked out (m) has four added to it which equals the total cost (c) he will have to pay.

13. C: This is a simple addition problem. Line up the decimals so that they are all in the same place in the equation, and see that there is a 3 by itself in the hundredths column. Then add the tenths column: 6+3+5 to get 14. Write down the 4 and carry the 1. Add the ones column: 3 plus the carried 1. Write down 4. Then write down the 1.

14. B: Anna's piece and Bonnie's piece need to be added together. To add fractions, the denominators need to be the same. Since 2 can be multiplied by a factor of 2 to equal 4, multiply the numerator and denominator by 2 to create an equivalent fraction with a like denominator: $\frac{1}{2} = \frac{2}{4}$. Add the numerators, but leave the denominators the same: $\frac{2}{4} + \frac{1}{4} = \frac{3}{4}$. Anna and Bonnie took a total of $\frac{3}{4}$ of the cake. To figure out how much Carol was left with, subtract $\frac{3}{4}$ from the whole: $1 - \frac{3}{4}$. The whole can also be represented as $\frac{4}{4}$ since our denominator is 4. Subtract the numerators, but leave the denominators the same: $\frac{4}{4} - \frac{3}{4} = \frac{1}{4}$. Therefore, Carol was left with $\frac{1}{4}$ of the cake.

15. D: Circle the 6 in the hundredths place. Look at the digit in the thousandths place. Since it is over 5, the 6 becomes 7.

16. A: First you need like denominators. For 6 and 8 that would be 24. $\frac{5}{8} = \frac{15}{24}$ and $\frac{5}{6} = \frac{20}{24}$. So, the second one is $\frac{5}{24}$ bigger.

17. C: The amount received by each employee is equal to the total amount of the bonus divided by the number of employees. The amount each employee receives equals $5,000 $\div$ 20 = $250.

18. D: Use the volume of a rectangular prism formula $V = L \times W \times H$ to determine the length of the tank.

$$200 = L \times 8 \times 5$$
$$200 = 40L$$
$$L = 5 \text{ feet}$$

19. C: Dividing the height of Mt. McKinley by the number of feet in a mile gives the correct result. $\frac{20320}{5280} = 3.85$ miles. This rounds to the approximation of 4 miles high.

20. A: Write 208. The word "and" represents the decimal point. Then write 402, and the last digit should match the correct place value. The 2 is in the thousandths place value, so it is correct.

21. D: Answer choice A defines raising the wholesale price by $1.75. Answer choice B defines multiplying the wholesale price by 0.25 and then adding $1.50. Answer choice C defines multiplying the wholesale price by 1.75.

22. C: The right section of the Venn diagram contains a shape with at least one right angle. The left section of the Venn diagram contains quadrilaterals that all have at least one set of parallel sides. The middle section of the Venn diagram contains polygons that have at least one right angle and have at least one set of parallel sides. Choice C is the only correct label for the section on the left.

Choice A is incorrect because none of the polygons on the left have right angles.

Choice B is incorrect because one of the polygons on the left does not have two sets of parallel sides.

Choice D is incorrect because none of the polygons on the left have at least three acute angles.

23. B: Order of operations are parentheses, exponents, multiplication, division, addition, and subtraction. The steps to solve this problem are:

$$3 + (9 - 4) \times (4 + 5)$$
$$3 + 5 \times 9$$
$$3 + 45$$
$$48$$

24. C: The train from Portland to Seattle is 145.8 miles. Craig needs to take the train from Portland to Seattle, and then from Seattle to Portland. This means that Craig will travel 145.8 + 145.8 miles. To add the decimal values, stack both numbers and line up the decimal points. Add each column from right to left. Regroup when necessary. The sum of $145.8 + 145.8$ is 291.6. Therefore, Craig traveled 291.6 miles.

$$\begin{array}{r} \scriptstyle 1\;1\;\; \\ 145.8 \\ +145.8 \\ \hline 291.6 \end{array}$$

25. The input-output table displays x-values and y-values that form ordered pairs. The ordered pairs listed in the input-output table are (10,6), (11,12), (12,18), and (13, 24). x-values are listed first, and y-values are listed second: (x, y). x-values are located along the horizontal axis, and y-values are located along the vertical axis. To plot the point (10,6), start at the origin and move 10 places to the right and then 6 places up. Use the same process for the other three points.

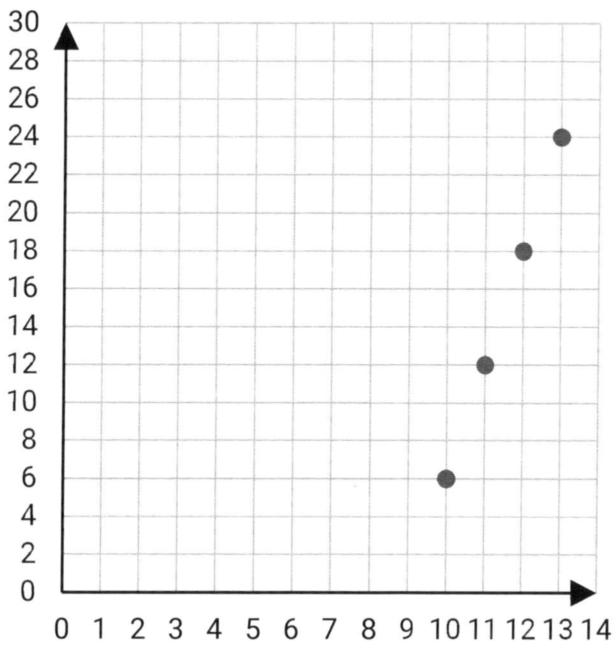

26. C: The order of operations, or PEMDAS, is a reference to the correct order in which to simplify a numerical expression. PEMDAS refers to parentheses, exponents, multiplication & division, and addition & subtraction. In the expression $[60(20 - 3)] + 1$, the math within the parentheses should be simplified first. In this case, 3 is subtracted from 20. The next step is to multiply the result by 60. The last step is to add 1.

27. B: On the plane provided, north is up and west is to the left. Shift point (8,5) up 2 and left 4 units to obtain the position of the fire. Thus, the fire is at (4,7) on the coordinate plane.

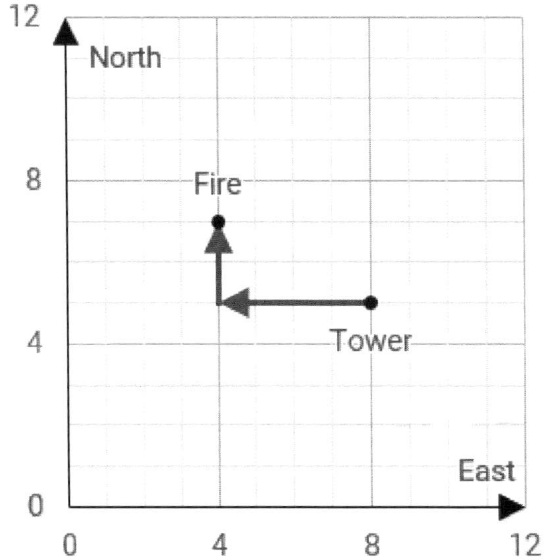

28. D: A box that is $13 \times 4 \times 8$ would be 416 cubic inches.

29. C: The total amount of brown sugar used for the cakes is 3 cups. Each cake required $\frac{1}{4}$ cup of brown sugar. To determine the number of cakes, divide each cup of brown sugar into groups of $\frac{1}{4}$. 3 cups divided into groups of $\frac{1}{4}$ results in 12 groups. Rylie baked 12 cakes for the fundraiser.

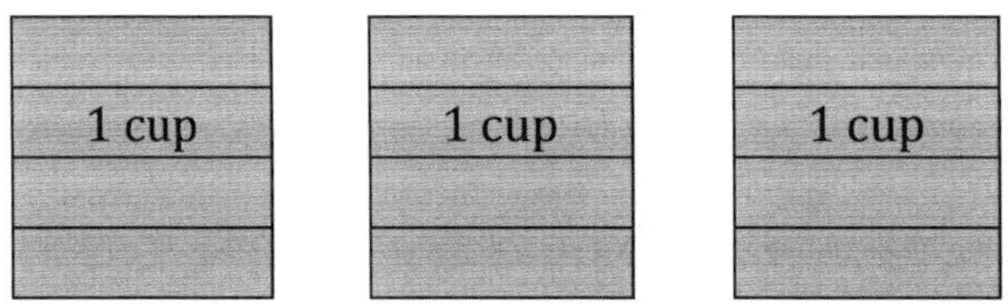

30. D: Multiply the decimals together using the standard algorithm. Then move the decimal over four places from the far right since there is a total of 4 places behind the decimals values.

$$\begin{array}{r} 0.28 \\ \times\ \underline{0.17} \\ 0.0476 \end{array}$$

31. B: Chef Xi bakes 6 pies every hour, for 4 hours. This can be expresses as (6×4).

Chef Shi bakes twice as many pies as Chef Xi. This can be expressed as $2(6 \times 4)$.

The host of the celebration has 7 pies, in addition to the pies that Chef Xi and Chef Shi contribute. This is expressed as $2(6 \times 4) + (6 \times 4) + 7$.

32. B, C: Choices B and C correctly describe the origin of a coordinate plane. Choice A is not correct because not all lines pass through the origin. Choice D describes the first quadrant of a graph. The first quadrant of a graph is not the same thing as the origin of a graph. Choice E is incorrect because two lines may intersect at any point, not just the origin.

33. C: Each bag of popcorn costs \$3.90, and Frank sells 3 bags. This simplifies to 3×3.9. Each hotdog costs \$2.50, and Frank sells 2. This simplifies to 2×2.5. The total cost is calculated by finding the sum of 3×3.9 and 2×2.5. The equation $c = 3(3.9) + 2(2.5)$ represents the scenario. To solve for the variable c, multiply 3 by 3.9, and 2 by 2.5.

$$3 \times 3.9 = 11.7$$
$$2 \times 2.5 = 5$$

The sum of 11.7 and 5 is 16.7. This represents \$16.70. The customer spent \$16.70 and paid with four 5-dollar bills. This means that the customer paid \$20 for a purchase of \$16.70. Subtract to calculate the customer's change, $20.00 - 16.70 = 3.30$. The customer will receive \$3.30 in change.

34. D: The expression $\frac{1}{7} \div 3$ can be modeled by shading in $\frac{1}{7}$ of a whole.

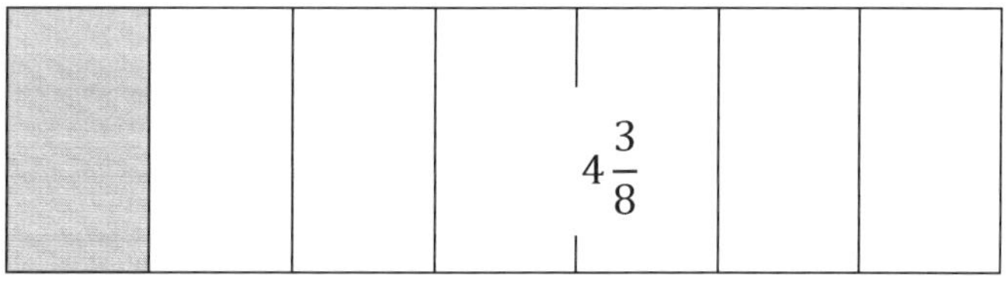

and then dividing this shaded region into 3 equal shares. Each share represents $\frac{1}{21}$ of the whole: $\frac{1}{7} \div 3 = \frac{1}{21}$.

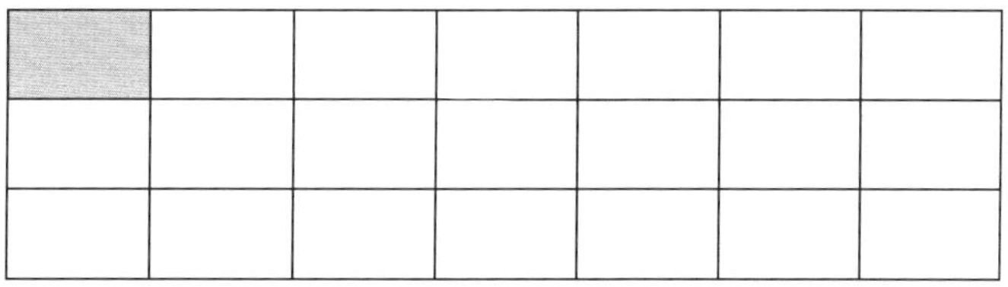

35. B: The four choices are marked on the diagram below. The only ordered pair that lies inside the enclosed region is (8,9).

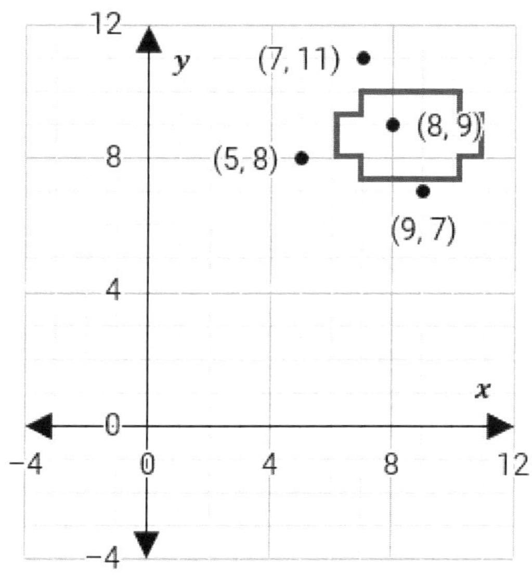

36. C: The area of a rectangle is the product of its length by its width. Since the length and width are given, multiply the two mixed numbers together. In order to multiply, the mixed numbers must be converted to improper fractions. Then multiply the numerators together, and multiply the denominators together. Finally, simplify and convert back to a mixed number.

$$3\frac{2}{5} \times 5\frac{7}{10} = \frac{17}{5} \times \frac{57}{10} = \frac{969}{50} = 19\frac{19}{50}$$

37. B: The volume of a rectangular prism can be calculated as the product of its length, width, and height. The formula $V = l \times w \times h$ can be applied in this scenario. The length of the prism is 4 units. The width of the prism is 8 units. The height of the prism is 5 units.

$V = l \times w \times h$ becomes $V = 4 \times 8 \times 5$, which simplifies to 160 cubic units. The units are *cubic* because three dimensions are multiplied.

38. D: To compare decimal numbers, we compare them at the most significant place, the leftmost place, at which they differ. All three numbers have the same digit, 2, in the tenths place, so we move to the hundredths place. In the hundredths place, $0.2\underline{4}$ has a 4, which is larger than the 3 in the hundredths place of both $0.2\underline{3}7$ and $0.2\underline{3}66$, so 0.24 is the largest number. To compare 0.237 and 0.2366 we next look at the thousandths place, where the 7 in $0.23\underline{7}$ is larger than the 6 in $0.23\underline{6}6$. So, 0.237 is greater than 0.2366. Thus, $0.2366 < 0.237 < 0.24$.

39. A: Write 512 then add the decimal in the thousandths place, the third place from the right.

40. A: When multiplying whole numbers by fractions, give the whole number a denominator of 1. Multiply the numerators together. Then multiply the denominators together. The last step is to simplify the fraction. Since the product was an improper fraction, the simplified answer will be a mixed number. Perform division to convert it to a mixed number. The remainder will be put over the original denominator. Then that fraction must be put in simplest form if it is not already in it.

$$3 \times \frac{6}{7} = \frac{3}{1} \times \frac{6}{7} = \frac{18}{7} = 2\frac{4}{7}$$

How to Overcome Test Anxiety

Just the thought of taking a test is enough to make most people a little nervous. A test is an important event that can have a long-term impact on your future, so it's important to take it seriously and it's natural to feel anxious about performing well. But just because anxiety is normal, that doesn't mean that it's helpful in test taking, or that you should simply accept it as part of your life. Anxiety can have a variety of effects. These effects can be mild, like making you feel slightly nervous, or severe, like blocking your ability to focus or remember even a simple detail.

If you experience test anxiety—whether severe or mild—it's important to know how to beat it. To discover this, first you need to understand what causes test anxiety.

Causes of Test Anxiety

While we often think of anxiety as an uncontrollable emotional state, it can actually be caused by simple, practical things. One of the most common causes of test anxiety is that a person does not feel adequately prepared for their test. This feeling can be the result of many different issues such as poor study habits or lack of organization, but the most common culprit is time management. Starting to study too late, failing to organize your study time to cover all of the material, or being distracted while you study will mean that you're not well prepared for the test. This may lead to cramming the night before, which will cause you to be physically and mentally exhausted for the test. Poor time management also contributes to feelings of stress, fear, and hopelessness as you realize you are not well prepared but don't know what to do about it.

Other times, test anxiety is not related to your preparation for the test but comes from unresolved fear. This may be a past failure on a test, or poor performance on tests in general. It may come from comparing yourself to others who seem to be performing better or from the stress of living up to expectations. Anxiety may be driven by fears of the future—how failure on this test would affect your educational and career goals. These fears are often completely irrational, but they can still negatively impact your test performance.

Elements of Test Anxiety

As mentioned earlier, test anxiety is considered to be an emotional state, but it has physical and mental components as well. Sometimes you may not even realize that you are suffering from test anxiety until you notice the physical symptoms. These can include trembling hands, rapid heartbeat, sweating, nausea, and tense muscles. Extreme anxiety may lead to fainting or vomiting. Obviously, any of these symptoms can have a negative impact on testing. It is important to recognize them as soon as they begin to occur so that you can address the problem before it damages your performance.

The mental components of test anxiety include trouble focusing and inability to remember learned information. During a test, your mind is on high alert, which can help you recall information and stay focused for an extended period of time. However, anxiety interferes with your mind's natural processes, causing you to blank out, even on the questions you know well. The strain of testing during anxiety makes it difficult to stay focused, especially on a test that may take several hours. Extreme anxiety can take a huge mental toll, making it difficult not only to recall test information but even to understand the test questions or pull your thoughts together.

Effects of Test Anxiety

Test anxiety is like a disease—if left untreated, it will get progressively worse. Anxiety leads to poor performance, and this reinforces the feelings of fear and failure, which in turn lead to poor performances on subsequent tests. It can grow from a mild nervousness to a crippling condition. If allowed to progress, test anxiety can have a big impact on your schooling, and consequently on your future.

Test anxiety can spread to other parts of your life. Anxiety on tests can become anxiety in any stressful situation, and blanking on a test can turn into panicking in a job situation. But fortunately, you don't have to let anxiety rule your testing and determine your grades. There are a number of relatively simple steps you can take to move past anxiety and function normally on a test and in the rest of life.

Physical Steps for Beating Test Anxiety

While test anxiety is a serious problem, the good news is that it can be overcome. It doesn't have to control your ability to think and remember information. While it may take time, you can begin taking steps today to beat anxiety.

Just as your first hint that you may be struggling with anxiety comes from the physical symptoms, the first step to treating it is also physical. Rest is crucial for having a clear, strong mind. If you are tired, it is much easier to give in to anxiety. But if you establish good sleep habits, your body and mind will be ready to perform optimally, without the strain of exhaustion. Additionally, sleeping well helps you to retain information better, so you're more likely to recall the answers when you see the test questions.

Getting good sleep means more than going to bed on time. It's important to allow your brain time to relax. Take study breaks from time to time so it doesn't get overworked, and don't study right before bed. Take time to rest your mind before trying to rest your body, or you may find it difficult to fall asleep.

Along with sleep, other aspects of physical health are important in preparing for a test. Good nutrition is vital for good brain function. Sugary foods and drinks may give a burst of energy but this burst is followed by a crash, both physically and emotionally. Instead, fuel your body with protein and vitamin-rich foods.

Also, drink plenty of water. Dehydration can lead to headaches and exhaustion, especially if your brain is already under stress from the rigors of the test. Particularly if your test is a long one, drink water during the breaks. And if possible, take an energy-boosting snack to eat between sections.

Along with sleep and diet, a third important part of physical health is exercise. Maintaining a steady workout schedule is helpful, but even taking 5-minute study breaks to walk can help get your blood pumping faster and clear your head. Exercise also releases endorphins, which contribute to a positive feeling and can help combat test anxiety.

When you nurture your physical health, you are also contributing to your mental health. If your body is healthy, your mind is much more likely to be healthy as well. So take time to rest, nourish your body with healthy food and water, and get moving as much as possible. Taking these physical steps will make you stronger and more able to take the mental steps necessary to overcome test anxiety.

Mental Steps for Beating Test Anxiety

Working on the mental side of test anxiety can be more challenging, but as with the physical side, there are clear steps you can take to overcome it. As mentioned earlier, test anxiety often stems from lack of preparation, so the obvious solution is to prepare for the test. Effective studying may be the most important weapon you have for beating test anxiety, but you can and should employ several other mental tools to combat fear.

First, boost your confidence by reminding yourself of past success—tests or projects that you aced. If you're putting as much effort into preparing for this test as you did for those, there's no reason you should expect to fail here. Work hard to prepare; then trust your preparation.

Second, surround yourself with encouraging people. It can be helpful to find a study group, but be sure that the people you're around will encourage a positive attitude. If you spend time with others who are anxious or cynical, this will only contribute to your own anxiety. Look for others who are motivated to study hard from a desire to succeed, not from a fear of failure.

Third, reward yourself. A test is physically and mentally tiring, even without anxiety, and it can be helpful to have something to look forward to. Plan an activity following the test, regardless of the outcome, such as going to a movie or getting ice cream.

When you are taking the test, if you find yourself beginning to feel anxious, remind yourself that you know the material. Visualize successfully completing the test. Then take a few deep, relaxing breaths and return to it. Work through the questions carefully but with confidence, knowing that you are capable of succeeding.

Developing a healthy mental approach to test taking will also aid in other areas of life. Test anxiety affects more than just the actual test—it can be damaging to your mental health and even contribute to depression. It's important to beat test anxiety before it becomes a problem for more than testing.

Study Strategy

Being prepared for the test is necessary to combat anxiety, but what does being prepared look like? You may study for hours on end and still not feel prepared. What you need is a strategy for test prep. The next few pages outline our recommended steps to help you plan out and conquer the challenge of preparation.

Step 1: Scope Out the Test

Learn everything you can about the format (multiple choice, essay, etc.) and what will be on the test. Gather any study materials, course outlines, or sample exams that may be available. Not only will this help you to prepare, but knowing what to expect can help to alleviate test anxiety.

Step 2: Map Out the Material

Look through the textbook or study guide and make note of how many chapters or sections it has. Then divide these over the time you have. For example, if a book has 15 chapters and you have five days to study, you need to cover three chapters each day. Even better, if you have the time, leave an extra day at the end for overall review after you have gone through the material in depth.

If time is limited, you may need to prioritize the material. Look through it and make note of which sections you think you already have a good grasp on, and which need review. While you are studying, skim quickly through the familiar sections and take more time on the challenging parts.

Write out your plan so you don't get lost as you go. Having a written plan also helps you feel more in control of the study, so anxiety is less likely to arise from feeling overwhelmed at the amount to cover.

Step 3: Gather Your Tools

Decide what study method works best for you. Do you prefer to highlight in the book as you study and then go back over the highlighted portions? Or do you type out notes of the important information? Or is it helpful to make flashcards that you can carry with you? Assemble the pens, index cards, highlighters, post-it notes, and any other materials you may need so you won't be distracted by getting up to find things while you study.

If you're having a hard time retaining the information or organizing your notes, experiment with different methods. For example, try color-coding by subject with colored pens, highlighters, or post-it notes. If you learn better by hearing, try recording yourself reading your notes so you can listen while in the car, working out, or simply sitting at your desk. Ask a friend to quiz you from your flashcards, or try teaching someone the material to solidify it in your mind.

Step 4: Create Your Environment

It's important to avoid distractions while you study. This includes both the obvious distractions like visitors and the subtle distractions like an uncomfortable chair (or a too-comfortable couch that makes you want to fall asleep). Set up the best study environment possible: good lighting and a comfortable work area. If background music helps you focus, you may want to turn it on, but otherwise keep the room quiet. If you are using a computer to take notes, be sure you don't have any other windows open, especially applications like social media, games, or anything else that could distract you. Silence your phone and turn off notifications. Be sure to keep water close by so you stay hydrated while you study (but avoid unhealthy drinks and snacks).

Also, take into account the best time of day to study. Are you freshest first thing in the morning? Try to set aside some time then to work through the material. Is your mind clearer in the afternoon or evening? Schedule your study session then. Another method is to study at the same time of day that you will take the test, so that your brain gets used to working on the material at that time and will be ready to focus at test time.

Step 5: Study!

Once you have done all the study preparation, it's time to settle into the actual studying. Sit down, take a few moments to settle your mind so you can focus, and begin to follow your study plan. Don't give in to distractions or let yourself procrastinate. This is your time to prepare so you'll be ready to fearlessly approach the test. Make the most of the time and stay focused.

Of course, you don't want to burn out. If you study too long you may find that you're not retaining the information very well. Take regular study breaks. For example, taking five minutes out of every hour to walk briskly, breathing deeply and swinging your arms, can help your mind stay fresh.

As you get to the end of each chapter or section, it's a good idea to do a quick review. Remind yourself of what you learned and work on any difficult parts. When you feel that you've mastered the material, move on to the next part. At the end of your study session, briefly skim through your notes again.

But while review is helpful, cramming last minute is NOT. If at all possible, work ahead so that you won't need to fit all your study into the last day. Cramming overloads your brain with more information than it can process and retain, and your tired mind may struggle to recall even previously learned information when it is overwhelmed with last-minute study. Also, the urgent nature of cramming and the stress placed on your brain contribute to anxiety. You'll be more likely to go to the test feeling unprepared and having trouble thinking clearly.

So don't cram, and don't stay up late before the test, even just to review your notes at a leisurely pace. Your brain needs rest more than it needs to go over the information again. In fact, plan to finish your studies by noon or early afternoon the day before the test. Give your brain the rest of the day to relax or focus on other things, and get a good night's sleep. Then you will be fresh for the test and better able to recall what you've studied.

Step 6: Take a Practice Test

Many courses offer sample tests, either online or in the study materials. This is an excellent resource to check whether you have mastered the material, as well as to prepare for the test format and environment.

Check the test format ahead of time: the number of questions, the type (multiple choice, free response, etc.), and the time limit. Then create a plan for working through them. For example, if you have 30 minutes to take a 60-question test, your limit is 30 seconds per question. Spend less time on the questions you know well so that you can take more time on the difficult ones.

If you have time to take several practice tests, take the first one open book, with no time limit. Work through the questions at your own pace and make sure you fully understand them. Gradually work up to taking a test under test conditions: sit at a desk with all study materials put away and set a timer. Pace yourself to make sure you finish the test with time to spare and go back to check your answers if you have time.

After each test, check your answers. On the questions you missed, be sure you understand why you missed them. Did you misread the question (tests can use tricky wording)? Did you forget the information? Or was it something you hadn't learned? Go back and study any shaky areas that the practice tests reveal.

Taking these tests not only helps with your grade, but also aids in combating test anxiety. If you're already used to the test conditions, you're less likely to worry about it, and working through tests until you're scoring well gives you a confidence boost. Go through the practice tests until you feel comfortable, and then you can go into the test knowing that you're ready for it.

Test Tips

On test day, you should be confident, knowing that you've prepared well and are ready to answer the questions. But aside from preparation, there are several test day strategies you can employ to maximize your performance.

First, as stated before, get a good night's sleep the night before the test (and for several nights before that, if possible). Go into the test with a fresh, alert mind rather than staying up late to study.

Try not to change too much about your normal routine on the day of the test. It's important to eat a nutritious breakfast, but if you normally don't eat breakfast at all, consider eating just a protein bar. If you're a coffee drinker, go ahead and have your normal coffee. Just make sure you time it so that the caffeine doesn't wear off right in the middle of your test. Avoid sugary beverages, and drink enough water to stay hydrated but not so much that you need a restroom break 10 minutes into the test. If your test isn't first thing in the morning, consider going for a walk or doing a light workout before the test to get your blood flowing.

Allow yourself enough time to get ready, and leave for the test with plenty of time to spare so you won't have the anxiety of scrambling to arrive in time. Another reason to be early is to select a good seat. It's helpful to sit away from doors and windows, which can be distracting. Find a good seat, get out your supplies, and settle your mind before the test begins.

When the test begins, start by going over the instructions carefully, even if you already know what to expect. Make sure you avoid any careless mistakes by following the directions.

Then begin working through the questions, pacing yourself as you've practiced. If you're not sure on an answer, don't spend too much time on it, and don't let it shake your confidence. Either skip it and come back later, or eliminate as many wrong answers as possible and guess among the remaining ones. Don't dwell on these questions as you continue—put them out of your mind and focus on what lies ahead.

Be sure to read all of the answer choices, even if you're sure the first one is the right answer. Sometimes you'll find a better one if you keep reading. But don't second-guess yourself if you do immediately know the answer. Your gut instinct is usually right. Don't let test anxiety rob you of the information you know.

If you have time at the end of the test (and if the test format allows), go back and review your answers. Be cautious about changing any, since your first instinct tends to be correct, but make sure you didn't misread any of the questions or accidentally mark the wrong answer choice. Look over any you skipped and make an educated guess.

At the end, leave the test feeling confident. You've done your best, so don't waste time worrying about your performance or wishing you could change anything. Instead, celebrate the successful completion of this test. And finally, use this test to learn how to deal with anxiety even better next time.

Review Video: Test Anxiety
Visit mometrix.com/academy and enter code: 100340

Important Qualification

Not all anxiety is created equal. If your test anxiety is causing major issues in your life beyond the classroom or testing center, or if you are experiencing troubling physical symptoms related to your anxiety, it may be a sign of a serious physiological or psychological condition. If this sounds like your situation, we strongly encourage you to seek professional help.

How to Overcome Your Fear of Math

Not again. You're sitting in math class, look down at your test, and immediately start to panic. Your stomach is in knots, your heart is racing, and you break out in a cold sweat. You're staring at the paper, but everything looks like it's written in a foreign language. Even though you studied, you're blanking out on how to begin solving these problems.

Does this sound familiar? If so, then you're not alone! You may be like millions of other people who experience math anxiety. Anxiety about performing well in math is a common experience for students of all ages. In this article, we'll discuss what math anxiety is, common misconceptions about learning math, and tips and strategies for overcoming math anxiety.

What Is Math Anxiety?

Psychologist Mark H. Ashcraft explains math anxiety as a feeling of tension, apprehension, or fear that interferes with math performance. Having math anxiety negatively impacts people's beliefs about themselves and what they can achieve. It hinders achievement within the math classroom and affects the successful application of mathematics in the real world.

Symptoms and Signs of Math Anxiety

To overcome math anxiety, you must recognize its symptoms. Becoming aware of the signs of math anxiety is the first step in addressing and resolving these fears.

Negative Self-Talk

If you have math anxiety, you've most likely said at least one of these statements to yourself:

- "I hate math."
- "I'm not good at math."
- "I'm not a math person."

The way we speak to ourselves and think about ourselves matters. Our thoughts become our words, our words become our actions, and our actions become our habits. Thinking negatively about math creates a self-fulfilling prophecy. In other words, if you take an idea as a fact, then it will come true because your behaviors will align to match it.

Avoidance

Some people who are fearful or anxious about math will tend to avoid it altogether. Avoidance can manifest in the following ways:

- Lack of engagement with math content
- Not completing homework and other assignments
- Not asking for help when needed
- Skipping class
- Avoiding math-related courses and activities

Avoidance is one of the most harmful impacts of math anxiety. If you steer clear of math at all costs, then you can't set yourself up for the success you deserve.

Lack of Motivation

Students with math anxiety may experience a lack of motivation. They may struggle to find the incentive to get engaged with what they view as a frightening subject. These students are often overwhelmed, making it difficult for them to complete or even start math assignments.

Procrastination

Another symptom of math anxiety is procrastination. Students may voluntarily delay or postpone their classwork and assignments, even if they know there will be a negative consequence for doing so. Additionally, they may choose to wait until the last minute to start projects and homework, even when they know they need more time to put forth their best effort.

Physiological Reactions

Many people with a fear of math experience physiological side effects. These may include an increase in heart rate, sweatiness, shakiness, nausea, and irregular breathing. These symptoms make it difficult to focus on the math content, causing the student even more stress and fear.

Strong Emotional Responses

Math anxiety also affects people on an emotional level. Responding to math content with strong emotions such as panic, anger, or despair can be a sign of math anxiety.

Low Test Scores and Performance

Low achievement can be both a symptom and a cause of math anxiety. When someone does not take the steps needed to perform well on tests and assessments, they are less likely to pass. The more they perform poorly, the more they accept this poor performance as a fact that can't be changed.

Feeling Alone

People who experience math anxiety feel like they are the only ones struggling, even if the math they are working on is challenging to many people. Feeling isolated in what they perceive as failure can trigger tension or nervousness.

Feeling of Permanency

Math anxiety can feel very permanent. You may assume that you are naturally bad at math and always will be. Viewing math as a natural ability rather than a skill that can be learned causes people to believe that nothing will help them improve. They take their current math abilities as fact and assume that they can't be changed. As a result, they give up, stop trying to improve, and avoid engaging with math altogether.

Lack of Confidence

People with low self-confidence in math tend to feel awkward and incompetent when asked to solve a math problem. They don't feel comfortable taking chances or risks when problem-solving because they second-guess themselves and assume they are incorrect. They don't trust in their ability to learn the content and solve problems correctly.

Panic

A general sense of unexplained panic is also a sign of math anxiety. You may feel a sudden sense of fear that triggers physical reactions, even when there is no apparent reason for such a response.

Causes Of Math Anxiety

Math anxiety can start at a young age and may have one or more underlying causes. Common causes of math anxiety include the following:

The Attitude of Parents or Guardians

Parents often put pressure on their children to perform well in school. Although their intentions are usually good, this pressure can lead to anxiety, especially if the student is struggling with a subject or class.

Perhaps your parents or others in your life hold negative predispositions about math based on their own experiences. For instance, if your mother once claimed she was not good at math, then you might have incorrectly interpreted this as a predisposed trait that was passed down to you.

Teacher Influence

Students often pick up on their teachers' attitudes about the content being taught. If a teacher is happy and excited about math, students are more likely to mirror these emotions. However, if a teacher lacks enthusiasm or genuine interest, then students are more inclined to disengage.

Teachers have a responsibility to cultivate a welcoming classroom culture that is accepting of mistakes. When teachers blame students for not understanding a concept, they create a hostile classroom environment where mistakes are not tolerated. This tension increases student stress and anxiety, creating conditions that are not conducive to inquiry and learning. Instead, when teachers normalize mistakes as a natural part of the problem-solving process, they give their students the freedom to explore and grapple with the math content. In such an environment, students feel comfortable taking chances because they are not afraid of being wrong.

Students need teachers that can help when they're having problems understanding difficult concepts. In doing so, educators may need to change how they teach the content. Since different people have unique learning styles, it's the job of the teacher to adapt to the needs of each student. Additionally, teachers should encourage students to explore alternate problem-solving strategies, even if it's not the preferred method of the educator.

Fear of Being Wrong

Embarrassing situations can be traumatic, especially for young children and adolescents. These experiences can stay with people through their adult lives. Those with math anxiety may experience a fear of being wrong, especially in front of a group of peers. This fear can be paralyzing, interfering with the student's concentration and ability to focus on the problem at hand.

Timed Assessments

Timed assessments can help improve math fluency, but they often create unnecessary pressure for students to complete an unrealistic number of problems within a specified timeframe. Many studies have shown that timed assessments often result in increased levels of anxiety, reducing a student's overall competence and ability to problem-solve.

Debunking Math Myths

There are lots of myths about math that are related to the causes and development of math-related anxiety. Although these myths have been proven to be false, many people take them as fact. Let's go over a few of the most common myths about learning math.

Myth: Men Are Better at Math Than Women

Math has a reputation for being a male-dominant subject, but this doesn't mean that men are inherently better at math than women. Many famous mathematical discoveries have been made by women. Katherine Johnson, Dame Mary Lucy Cartwright, and Marjorie Lee Brown are just a few of the many famous women mathematicians. Expecting to be good or bad at math because of your gender sets you up for stress and confusion. Math is a skill that can be learned, just like cooking or riding a bike.

Myth: There Is Only One Good Way to Solve Math Problems

There are many ways to get the correct answer when it comes to math. No two people have the same brain, so everyone takes a slightly different approach to problem-solving. Moreover, there isn't one way of problem-solving that's superior to another. Your way of working through a problem might differ from someone else's, and that is okay. Math can be a highly individualized process, so the best method for you should be the one that makes you feel the most comfortable and makes the most sense to you.

Myth: Math Requires a Good Memory

For many years, mathematics was taught through memorization. However, learning in such a way hinders the development of critical thinking and conceptual understanding. These skill sets are much more valuable than basic memorization. For instance, you might be great at memorizing mathematical formulas, but if you don't understand what they mean, then you can't apply them to different scenarios in the real world. When a student is working from memory, they are limited in the strategies available to them to problem-solve. In other words, they assume there is only one correct way to do the math, which is the method they memorized. Having a variety of problem-solving options can help students figure out which method works best for them. Additionally, it provides students with a better understanding of how and why certain mathematical strategies work. While memorization can be helpful in some instances, it is not an absolute requirement for mathematicians.

Myth: Math Is Not Creative

Math requires imagination and intuition. Contrary to popular belief, it is a highly creative field. Mathematical creativity can help in developing new ways to think about and solve problems. Many people incorrectly assume that all things are either creative or analytical. However, this black-and-white view is limiting because the field of mathematics involves both creativity and logic.

Myth: Math Isn't Supposed To Be Fun

Whoever told you that math isn't supposed to be fun is a liar. There are tons of math-based activities and games that foster friendly competition and engagement. Math is often best learned through play, and lots of mobile apps and computer games exemplify this.

Additionally, math can be an exceptionally collaborative and social experience. Studying or working through problems with a friend often makes the process a lot more fun. The excitement and satisfaction of solving a difficult problem with others is quite rewarding. Math can be fun if you look for ways to make it more collaborative and enjoyable.

Myth: Not Everyone Is Capable of Learning Math

There's no such thing as a "math person." Although many people think that you're either good at math or you're not, this is simply not true. Everyone is capable of learning and applying mathematics. However, not everyone learns the same way. Since each person has a different learning style, the trick is to find the strategies and learning tools that work best for you. Some people learn best through hands-on experiences, and others find success through the use of visual aids. Others are auditory learners and learn best by hearing and listening. When people are overwhelmed or feel that math is too hard, it's often because they haven't found the learning strategy that works best for them.

Myth: Good Mathematicians Work Quickly and Never Make Mistakes

There is no prize for finishing first in math. It's not a race, and speed isn't a measure of your ability. Good mathematicians take their time to ensure their work is accurate. As you gain more experience and practice, you will naturally become faster and more confident.

Additionally, everyone makes mistakes, including good mathematicians. Mistakes are a normal part of the problem-solving process, and they're not a bad thing. The important thing is that we take the time to learn from our mistakes, understand where our misconceptions are, and move forward.

Myth: You Don't Need Math in the Real World

Our day-to-day lives are so infused with mathematical concepts that we often don't even realize when we're using math in the real world. In fact, most people tend to underestimate how much we do math in our everyday lives. It's involved in an enormous variety of daily activities such as shopping, baking, finances, and gardening, as well as in many careers, including architecture, nursing, design, and sales.

Tips and Strategies for Overcoming Math Anxiety

If your anxiety is getting in the way of your level of mathematical engagement, then there are lots of steps you can take. Check out the strategies below to start building confidence in math today.

Focus on Understanding, Not Memorization

Don't drive yourself crazy trying to memorize every single formula or mathematical process. Instead, shift your attention to understanding concepts. Those who prioritize memorization over conceptual understanding tend to have lower achievement levels in math. Students who memorize may be able to complete some math, but they don't understand the process well enough to apply it to different situations. Memorization comes with time and practice, but it won't help alleviate math anxiety. On the other hand, conceptual understanding will give you the building blocks of knowledge you need to build up your confidence.

Replace Negative Self-Talk with Positive Self-Talk

Start to notice how you think about yourself. Whenever you catch yourself thinking something negative, try replacing that thought with a positive affirmation. Instead of continuing the negative thought, pause to reframe the situation. For ideas on how to get started, take a look at the table below:

Instead of thinking...	Try thinking...
"I can't do this math." "I'm not a math person."	"I'm up for the challenge, and I'm training my brain in math."
"This problem is too hard."	"This problem is hard, so this might take some time and effort. I know I can do this."
"I give up."	"What strategies can help me solve this problem?"
"I made a mistake, so I'm not good at this."	"Everyone makes mistakes. Mistakes help me to grow and understand."
"I'll never be smart enough."	"I can figure this out, and I am smart enough."

Practice Mindfulness

Practicing mindfulness and focusing on your breathing can help alleviate some of the physical symptoms of math anxiety. By taking deep breaths, you can remind your nervous system that you are not in immediate danger. Doing so will reduce your heart rate and help with any irregular breathing or shakiness. Taking the edge off of the physiological effects of anxiety will clear your mind, allowing your brain to focus its energy on problem-solving.

Do Some Math Every Day

Think about learning math as if you were learning a foreign language. If you don't use it, you lose it. If you don't practice your math skills regularly, you'll have a harder time achieving comprehension and fluency. Set some amount of time aside each day, even if it's just for a few minutes, to practice. It might take some discipline to build a habit around this, but doing so will help increase your mathematical self-assurance.

Use All of Your Resources

Everyone has a different learning style, and there are plenty of resources out there to support all learners. When you get stuck on a math problem, think about the tools you have access to, and use them when applicable. Such resources may include flashcards, graphic organizers, study guides, interactive notebooks, and peer study groups. All of these are great tools to accommodate your individual learning style. Finding the tools and resources that work for your learning style will give you the confidence you need to succeed.

Realize That You Aren't Alone

Remind yourself that lots of other people struggle with math anxiety, including teachers, nurses, and even successful mathematicians. You aren't the only one who panics when faced with a new or challenging problem. It's probably much more common than you think. Realizing that you aren't alone in your experience can help put some distance between yourself and the emotions you feel about math. It also helps to normalize the anxiety and shift your perspective.

Ask Questions

If there's a concept you don't understand and you've tried everything you can, then it's okay to ask for help! You can always ask your teacher or professor for help. If you're not learning math in a traditional classroom, you may want to join a study group, work with a tutor, or talk to your friends. More often than not, you aren't the only one of your peers who needs clarity on a mathematical concept. Seeking understanding is a great way to increase self-confidence in math.

Remember That There's More Than One Way To Solve A Problem

Since everyone learns differently, it's best to focus on understanding a math problem with an approach that makes sense to you. If the way it's being taught is confusing to you, don't give up. Instead, work to understand the problem using a different technique. There's almost always more than one problem-solving method when it comes to math. Don't get stressed if one of them doesn't make sense to you. Instead, shift your focus to what does make sense. Chances are high that you know more than you think you do.

Visualization

Visualization is the process of creating images in your mind's eye. Picture yourself as a successful, confident mathematician. Think about how you would feel and how you would behave. What would your work area look like? How would you organize your belongings? The more you focus on something, the more likely you are to achieve it. Visualizing teaches your brain that you can achieve whatever it is that you want. Thinking about success in mathematics will lead to acting like a successful mathematician. This, in turn, leads to actual success.

Focus on the Easiest Problems First

To increase your confidence when working on a math test or assignment, try solving the easiest problems first. Doing so will remind you that you are successful in math and that you do have what it takes. This process will increase your belief in yourself, giving you the confidence you need to tackle more complex problems.

Find a Support Group

A study buddy, tutor, or peer group can go a long way in decreasing math-related anxiety. Such support systems offer lots of benefits, including a safe place to ask questions, additional practice with mathematical concepts, and an understanding of other problem-solving explanations that may work better for you. Equipping yourself with a support group is one of the fastest ways to eliminate math anxiety.

Reward Yourself for Working Hard

Recognize the amount of effort you're putting in to overcome your math anxiety. It's not an easy task, so you deserve acknowledgement. Surround yourself with people who will provide you with the positive reinforcement you deserve.

Remember, You Can Do This!

Conquering a fear of math can be challenging, but there are lots of strategies that can help you out. Your own beliefs about your mathematical capabilities can limit your potential. Working toward a growth mindset can have a tremendous impact on decreasing math-related anxiety and building confidence. By knowing the symptoms of math anxiety and recognizing common misconceptions about learning math, you can develop a plan to address your fear of math. Utilizing the strategies discussed can help you overcome this anxiety and build the confidence you need to succeed.

Online Resources

Due to our efforts to try to keep this book to a manageable length, we've created a link that will give you access to all of your online resources:

mometrix.com/resources719/terranextg5math

It's Your Moment, Let's Celebrate It!

Share your story @mometrixtestpreparation